DALLAS HOLM

·THIS IS MY STORY·

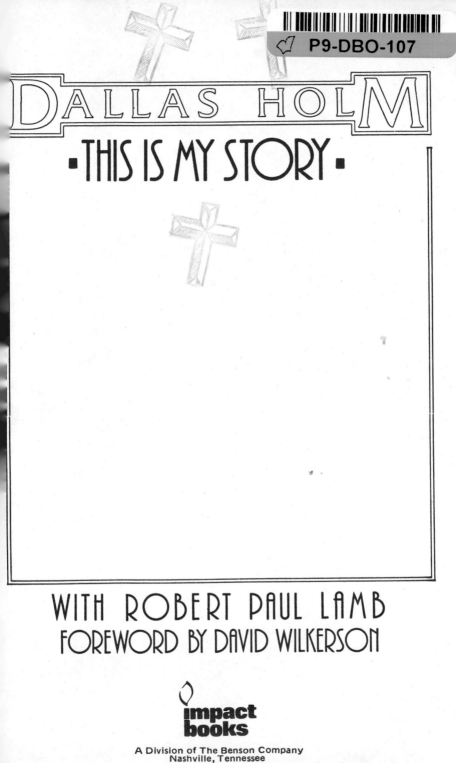

WITH ROBERT PAUL LAMB
FOREWORD BY DAVID WILKERSON

impact books

A Division of The Benson Company
Nashville, Tennessee

DALLAS HOLM

·THIS IS MY STORY·

Grateful acknowledgement is made by the author and publisher
for permission to quote Scripture passages from the following
sources:

HOLY BIBLE, New International Version, © copyright 1978,
New York Bible Society. Used by permission. Quotations
from this version are indicated by the abbreviation NIV in
parentheses.

New American Standard Bible, © copyright The Lockman
Foundation, 1960, 1962, 1963, 1971, 1972, 1973, 1975.
Used by permission. Quotations from this version are indicated
by the abbreviation NASB in parentheses.

Library of Congress Catalog Number: 80–81756

ISBN 0–914850–96–2

M0619

To my wonderful wife, Linda
whom I love more than words can say

TABLE OF CONTENTS

FOREWORD

Dallas Holm has become one of the most respected musical artists in the nation today. He has earned that respect because he is a devout and dedicated man of God.

In all the years Dallas has worked with me in crusades, I have never once heard him speak an unkind word. His humility is genuine and he is completely unaffected by his growing popularity.

Those of us who work with him closest, admire him most. He is not a performer or an entertainer, but rather, an apostle of love. When he sings and speaks, everyone in the audience knows he cares about them, as individuals. Money, success and recognition mean nothing to him. These words are not in his vocabulary. His single motivation is the salvation of the lost and the healing of hurts.

He was not a junkie or a gang leader. I know his parents and they are two of the loveliest Christians anywhere. But this is more than just the story of an ordinary boy from a good Christian home. It is the story of a dedicated young man who yielded his talent to Christ rather than squandering it in a rowdy rock world. It is the story of how God honors that kind of dedication.

I want my grandsons to grow up to be like Dallas.

DAVID WILKERSON
Twin Oaks Ranch, Texas

PREFACE

Without question, it takes a certain amount of curiosity, concern and genuine enthusiasm to project oneself into somebody else's shoes in the writing of their story. Having co-authored biographical works with such Christian personalities as evangelist Jimmy Swaggart, Jim Bakker of the "PTL Club," and several others, not so well-known, I have been down this road before. To be exact, this is my eleventh book of collaboration.

It would be easy to become jaded as I live other people's lives and witness all the un-glamorous moments behind the scenes. But that has not been the case with this book.

Whether Dallas Holm was singing to a packed coliseum audience in a David Wilkerson crusade in Jacksonville, Florida; or sharing his life in a crowded Baptist church in Fort Worth, Texas; or just relaxing in the quiet of his comfortable den in Lindale, Texas, I found him always the same—a soft-spoken, insightful man, full of dry wit, devoted to his family, and above all, deeply

dedicated to serving Jesus Christ. I was re-
freshed, challenged and encouraged by my ex-
posure to this man who walks so simply yet
profoundly with the Lord.

This Is My Story is the result of our collaboration. It is more than the success story of one of
America's finest contemporary vocalists and
songwriters—more than the froth and pulp that
sometimes appears under the banner of a well-
known Christian's testimony.

Dallas and his wife, Linda, have shared not
only their successes but their failures and frustrations as well—for that's how life truly is. They
have admitted honestly that they have not discovered any pat answers to the frequent turns
and twists of life. Instead, they have learned to
rely on the Lord in all circumstances. They have
learned that God, indeed, directs and guides us
in all our ways according to His own Master
Plan.

For all those who earnestly desire to walk the
Christian way, there is much to be gained from
this story. To those husbands and wives who
aspire to be teammates in the work of the Lord, I
encourage you to read the book, slowly savoring
the unfolding plan of God for Dallas and Linda
Holm.

This Is My Story is the pattern of God's deal-
ings with His people. As such, this is also *your*
story—and mine.

ROBERT PAUL LAMB
St. Simons Island,
Georgia

*"Delight yourself in the Lord;
and He will give you the desires
of your heart."*

Psalm 37:4

1

I'VE NEVER SEEN THE RIGHTEOUS FORSAKEN

O, I know you may get weary,
And the times, they may get rough;
You may not have all you want,
but you'll always have enough.
And when your darkest hour comes,
Just remember what I say:
I've never seen the righteous forsaken,
Or their seed begging for bread.

The doctor's words sounded sharp and startling like a heavy clap of thunder coming out of nowhere on a muggy summer day.

"We've found a large tumor in your wife's small intestine, Mr. Holm," he announced, shuffling some X-rays on his cluttered desk. "It can only be removed through major surgery."

Surgery.

The word sounded ominous and foreboding, conjuring up images of white-draped figures in surgical masks, laboring over some faceless form shrouded by mountains of sterile sheets. I could practically see the shiny green walls of the antiseptic operating room and hear the monotonous thumping and pumping of life support machines.

But this wasn't some television movie portrayed by actors on a screen. It was real life. And that person under the surgeon's knife would be my warm and vibrant wife, Linda—and the mother of our only child, Jennifer.

The doctor glanced at the calendar on his wristwatch. "We'll make arrangements for her to check into the hospital on Sunday afternoon and begin further tests on Monday."

Sunday was only two days away. Why so soon?

I didn't hear much of what the doctor was saying after that. My mind had already shifted into overdrive, considering the worst that could possibly happen. Why is it that the human mind, in spite of faith, so often seems to function that way? The tumor could be malignant. Her whole body could be riddled with cancer. She could die. What would happen then? to me? to Jennifer?

The doctor, a lean, tanned man with sharp features and thinning brown hair, obviously realized he had caught us off-guard.

"There is no real cause for alarm, Mr. and Mrs. Holm," he said. "With this particular disease, the polyps or tumors are almost never malignant."

Almost never. So what were the percentages? I could only nod miserably.

Linda was quiet, subdued.

We had heard similar medical assurances before. They didn't mean very much at that moment. All that registered was that Linda's recurring problem had not been solved. Only the doctors and nurses had changed. The diagnosis was the same. Linda was facing surgery—again.

She didn't say much but clutched my hand tightly as we walked out of the doctor's office and took the elevator to the street floor.

I crawled into the driver's seat of our Chevy van and looked over at Linda. Her head was pressed against the back of the seat and her eyes were closed.

"Do you think we ought to pray about this— now?" I asked.

"Yes," she sighed, resignation in her voice.

"Lord, we don't know what all this means," I began slowly, "but we trust You. We believe You can still heal Linda. We believe all things are possible with You, but . . ."

I choked and glanced at Linda. Her whole body was trembling and her eyes filled with tears. We fell into each other's arms. She cried out of fear and frustration. I cried because my precious wife was facing another operation and there wasn't a thing in the world I could do about it. I felt completely helpless.

The mysterious stomach disorder had plagued Linda for years. A week after we married, she suffered an attack and wound up in the hospital for several days. Throughout our married life, there had been one problem after another with the perplexing pains. At times, in the early hours of the morning, I would find her curled up on the bathroom floor, praying that the stabbing pains would pass.

Finally, in desperation, she agreed to see a

doctor. X-rays showed polyps in Linda's lower intestine.

"We'll have to operate," the doctor, an older man with jowled face and thick glasses, had said abruptly.

But we were not willing to settle for one opinion. In checking with Linda's father, who suffered with the same strange malady, a rare, hereditary disease of the intestinal tract, we learned of a process called fiber-optics in which polyps are removed without major surgery. As a chiropractor, he had connections with the excellent medical facility at the University of Minnesota.

We agreed that this should be the next step. So Linda flew to Minnesota for the relatively minor surgical procedure. The polyps were removed without complications and, within a matter of days, she was winging her way back to Texas.

"I'm sure glad *that's* settled," I said with relief when she arrived home.

"Yeah, me too," she smiled as she gave me a big hug. "Now maybe we can settle down to normal living."

But the problem *wasn't* solved. The stabbing pains, attacking suddenly like the sharp point of a razor, returned worse than before. I continued to pray to the God who had given so much to me and my family.

He had given me a role as a crusade soloist with Dave Wilkerson, known world-wide from his experiences in *The Cross and the Switchblade*. He'd given me best-selling records and the acclaim of thousands. Songs I'd written and recorded—like "Rise Again"—had hit the top of the gospel music charts. In 1978 alone, I had received four Doves, the most-coveted awards in gospel music.

Yet, as I sought God about the person I loved most in all the world, I continually met a brick wall. There seemed no way to crawl over, tunnel through, or go around the obstacle.

And it didn't make any sense. Linda and I were living for the Lord, serving Him in a full-time ministry. We had a solid marriage and a great family life. My only regret was that my heavy travel commitments kept us from spending more time together. But I was willing to make that sacrifice to do what I felt the Lord had called me to do. What I was *not* ready to give up—was Linda.

Joining in our prayers for her full healing were several families among the 75 people at Twin Oaks Ranch, just outside Lindale, Texas, where we live as part of David Wilkerson's World Challenge ministry.

Thursday nights on the ranch are special nights for those of us who are home between tours. It's the time when we who minister can dip our buckets into the well—a time for worship, a time for sharing, a time of prayer. For weeks, Linda's health had been the object of prayer among a few of our closest friends who knew about her condition. It was good to know that these people were praying—people we had come to love and trust. Linda and I firmly believed that "the prayer(s) of righteous (people) are powerful and effective" (Jas. 5:16, NIV). We were counting on them.

Yet, nothing anyone did seemed to ease Linda's pain. And it was the persistent, nagging pain that drove her to the specialist who had delivered the grim news on that Friday afternoon. Unless God gave Linda a miracle, she would have to undergo major surgery.

I suppose the gravity of the situation didn't actually sink in until Sunday afternoon when I checked her into the hospital. It was a gray, wet day. There was no turning back now. We made small talk for a few hours—avoiding the inevitable. Then, it was time for me to leave.

Linda's eyes were filled with fear and desperation. For a moment, I became lost in their empty green depths. I felt what she was feeling—an overwhelming sense of frustration.

Throughout our marriage, I had said goodbye to Linda many times, before leaving for every corner of the country and, occasionally, even overseas. But never was the word spoken with such difficulty as that first night when I left Linda alone in the hospital.

I drove the eighty miles from Dallas back to the ranch, weeping and talking to the Lord most of the way. The house was lonely and quiet when I pulled up. Always, Linda had been the one to remain at home while I traveled. Going into the empty house produced a peculiar feeling. I tried to keep busy. Then I tried to get some sleep. Nothing worked. I had never felt so low.

Sometimes, in the first shock of a crisis, God seems very far away, and getting through to Him, almost impossible. It wasn't that we felt God had let us down. It was just that we were so sure the minor surgery would correct Linda's problem. And now we were back at square one.

What do *you* do when you pray, really believing, and nothing seems to be happening? It helps to know that we don't wrestle with such questions by ourselves.

And we sensed that God was aware of our pain, our confusion, and even understood the guilt we felt as we questioned His purpose for Linda's suffering. Though I had prayed many times before, again it seemed the only thing to do. I just didn't know what to pray for.

O, I know it seems so hopeless,
and you don't know what to pray;
You've done all you know to do,
and it seems there's just no way;
And when you feel you're at the end,
Just remember what I say;
I've never seen the righteous forsaken,
Or their seed begging for bread!

Linda had more tests and X-rays on Monday. When I walked into her room Tuesday afternoon, the surgeon was standing over her bed with the results of the tests in his hand.

"I think we've located the problem," he said in greeting me. "It's a double intussusception of the intestine. Normally, in the case of an obstruction such as a tumor, the intestine telescopes, or folds over in an attempt to dislodge the foreign object. In Linda's case, however, we have found *two* folds."

"Really?" I responded with growing apprehension.

"That's not all," the doctor continued. "We've also found polyps in the stomach. In fact, there are so many it may be dangerous to try to remove them right now."

Linda's face appeared calm as we heard the news. I knew the full impact had not hit her. "We'll take a look at them when we operate tomorrow," he added, "and, if absolutely necessary, we'll remove them then."

Another blow. Not just one tumor in the intestine as we thought. Her stomach was loaded with polyps. Could those be malignant? *Oh, God, where are you?* I groaned to myself.

I stayed with Linda until the nine o'clock visitors' announcement came over the intercom. After praying with her, I returned to a nearby motel for the night.

When I got back to my room, it occurred to me that maybe I hadn't gotten specific enough with the Lord. Getting down on my knees beside the bed, I poured out my heart to the Lord, telling Him everything I was feeling. The fear of the surgery. The worry about Linda. The concern for myself and Jennifer should anything unexpected happen. I didn't hold anything back.

What followed was amazing. I can't say I heard a voice. I don't know that I've ever heard the audible voice of the Lord. But I know He spoke to me that night.

"You have two choices," He seemed to be saying. "You can have your miracle, if that's what you want. I can heal Linda tonight without surgery. Or, she can have the operation. There will be some pain. Her recovery will take about ten days. But in the process, you'll learn some things about each other, about yourselves, and about Me that you would never be able to learn any other way."

The choice was obvious. If Linda could be healed with just a simple prayer request, of course that was what I wanted.

But the still, small voice was insistent: "If you take the easy way, you'll be missing a valuable experience."

I struggled between the two impressions. How could I ask Linda to make such a sacrifice? It was her body, not mine. Why wouldn't I pray for healing if I *knew* my prayer would be answered? Yet, the Scriptures say we are all bought with a price. Our bodies don't belong to us; they belong to God. In that light, the decision was simple.

"Lord, I yield to you—to whatever You think is best for our lives. Our bodies are Yours. All that we have, all that we are, belongs to You. I only ask that You go through this experience with us. Let Your will be done."

The next day Linda underwent the surgery. The fist-sized tumor, which had caused the stabbing stomach pains, was removed, along with six inches of intestine. To our great relief, the tumor was not malignant.

During the next ten days, Linda recovered at such a rapid rate the doctors were astonished.

The dark clouds that had hovered over Linda ever since she learned that the polyp-producing disease was hereditary were gone! She was released from fear. Not that she will never again have a recurrence of the problem, but that God's all-sufficient love is available when we reach the end of our resources. Linda went into surgery knowing He was there just as surely as she knew

I would be waiting for her when she came out of the anesthetic. And that's really all she needed to know.

As for me, I felt she had been given back to me—like a gift. Life had never looked so good. Every minute together was new and precious. I had a feeling we would not be taking a lot of things for granted—like talking for hours at the kitchen table, or watching Jennifer blow out candles on a birthday cake, or eating cheeseburgers and buttered noodles at midnight!

Linda and I have always had a good marriage. It was difficult to believe that things could get any better. We have always been best friends— able to talk about everything and anything—or to be content saying nothing at all. There have never been any secrets between us, no jealousy, no game-playing.

The crisis only strengthened our communication. We shared our feelings honestly. We talked about our life together, our love for each other, examined fear in the light of faith. Sometimes we just held hands and cried together. I wanted to become a partner in her suffering.

And that's how I learned the greatest lesson of all. God does not always deliver us *from* painful situations, but He does always walk with us *through* them. He becomes a partner in our suffering! At the moment of my decision not to take the easy way out, He was also making a decision not to take the easy way. It would have been so simple for the Creator of the universe to work a quick miracle and be done with it. But He loved us too much for that. He chose, instead, to be "touched with the feeling of our infirmities." He willingly entered into our pain.

I've learned that the kind of faith that most pleases the Lord is the faith that says, *In the midst of our confusion, in the midst of not knowing what the future holds, in the midst of wondering whether our prayers are being heard—Father, we trust You anyway, we love You anyway, we believe in You anyway. It isn't necessary for us to understand anything more than this—You will never leave us or forsake us.*

So just hold on a little longer,
the answer's soon to come;
The endless waiting's almost over,
the victry's almost won.
And when again you feel His joy,
You'll remember what I said:
I've never seen the righteous forsaken,
*Or their seed begging for bread!**

2

ST. PAUL PARK

If a guy had to grow up in a small town, I guess St. Paul Park, Minnesota, is probably as nice a place as anywhere in the country. Located about ten miles south of St. Paul, the state capital, my hometown was about a mile or so from the Mississippi River, that giant body of water that begins as a quiet brook out of Lake Itasca in north central Minnesota and splits Minneapolis and St. Paul in half, rushing southward. St. Paul Park with its two thousand or so residents was home to me for the first twenty years of my life.

In the 1880's and 1890's, thousands of immigrants from the Scandinavian countries settled in America. Among them was Robert Holm, my grandfather, who was born in Denmark but migrated to Minnesota with his family at the age of four. Tena Hansen, my grandmother, was a native of Wisconsin, but her parents had come over from Denmark, too.

My father, Curt Holm, was raised in Wisconsin but moved to St. Paul Park in 1936 to work on a small dairy farm. He milked the cows in the morning, cooled and bottled the product, then peddled it from house to house. In one of the houses where he sold milk lived the Harbrecht family.

It was to this lively household that young Curt returned again and again for a glimpse of beautiful, bright-eyed Viola. Everybody called her "Tula" for short. Tula was the youngest daughter of Raymond and Sophia Harbrecht. The Harbrechts had met, married, and raised all five of their children in St. Paul Park. But Mrs. Harbrecht's roots, like those of so many other immigrants, were in Norway—the old country.

Curt enjoyed the warmth he found in that home and recognized that his family shared a common heritage with the Harbrechts. No other family on his route received such special deliveries! It wasn't long before Tula began to notice the handsome, young milkman.

Tula Harbrecht was an ardent churchgoer even as a teenager—the sparkplug of the youth group at St. Paul Park Church of God. Since she was there virtually "every time the doors opened," Curt found himself a fairly regular attender too. It wasn't that he was that keen on religion, but he sure didn't want to take any chances on losing the cutest little girl in St. Paul Park.

She was a feisty little thing—independent and outspoken. She reminded him of a high-spirited filly, tossing her golden-flecked brown hair whenever he teased her. No, he'd better stick around—and church was as good a place as any to do some courting.

Being the free spirit she was, Tula didn't see anything at all wrong with some of the "innocent" forms of recreation that the older, more conservative church members "frowned" on. It was after one of these outings that Pastor Max Gaulke called her aside one Sunday.

"Tula, I've been hearing some things that concern me deeply. I'd like to talk with you in my study. Could you come by one afternoon this week?"

"Of course. But everything's just fine, Pastor Gaulke," she smiled confidently.

Still, she was a little shaky about the conference and, when the day came, she persuaded Curt to go along. It was a day neither of them would be likely to forget.

Pastor Gaulke was one of God's great gifts to young people. His interest in them was based on an abiding belief in their potential. And when he saw some of the younger members of his flock ready to take a wrong turn, his great shepherd heart just reached out and drew them back into the fold.

Tula Harbrecht felt his sincere affection and faith in her that day before he ever opened his mouth. And when he did, his gentle admonition nearly broke her heart.

"Tula, you have so much to offer the Lord. Somehow, I feel that your commitment is not all it should be. Don't you think, my dear, that it's about time you decided once and for all to give *all* of your life to Christ?"

She dropped her proud, bright head. A tear slid down one cheek and dripped onto the floor of his study. Until that moment, Tula realized, she had been *in* the church, but not *of* it. God was asking more of her than her name on the church role and a lot of fervent activity. He wanted her heart and her life in a living, growing relationship with Him.

Curt, too, was having some second thoughts. He was getting pretty serious about this young lady and, if he were going to be the spiritual leader of their home, he would have to quit playing church.

"If the two of you will just be open, God has something more, something greater than either of you could ever dream. But you must be willing to go all the way with Him. Don't close Him out. He's waiting for you."

By this time, the three of them had slipped to their knees, weeping and praying. There would be no turning back.

Pastor Gaulke and God won two prizes for the Kingdom that day—my mother and father. Not too long afterwards, they were married. Now, theirs would be a real Christian home—all the way.

The young couple had only a few months to set up housekeeping before my dad was called to active military duty in the Army. By now, World War II was well underway and, in the Pacific, the Japanese forces were clashing cruelly with a remnant of McArthur's men in some of the hottest fighting of the war. General Douglas McArthur, himself, had been unceremoniously ordered out of the islands. His historic parting words to the Philippine people, "I shall return," was a promise he would keep. Dad had made the same promise to my mother.

Fortunately, he was not sent overseas immediately, but stayed stateside for basic training. He was assigned to the Army Infantry Detached Service as a surgical technician in the Medical Corps. Though he was transferred from one base to another, Mom managed to follow him around the country, sometimes riding all night on a crowded train so they could spend a few hours or days together.

When his sealed orders finally came, my mother discovered she was pregnant and went home to her parents to wait for Dad's return and for the birth of my brother, Doug.

A letter from Dad, written on Doug's first Christmas (before he was doing much reading) has a place of honor in Doug's baby book. Mom still can't read it without shedding a few tears—mostly because of God's goodness in returning Dad safely and for giving her a little son who looked just like him.

Dec. 25, 1945

Dear Son,

Just a few line to my first son from his dad who is away on this day—Christ's birthday.

May you live as Jesus did—clean and pure—a teacher of God's Word. Respect those who teach you. Help those whom you teach.

Always remember you have the best mother in the world. Never do a thing that will cause her pain.

Mother and Dad are proud of you, son, and have a lot of trust in you. Help us keep that trust.

All my love,
Dad

Dad spent only a few months more in the Philippines. By the time he arrived, the islands had been secured. With only small pockets of guerilla troops still hiding out in the mountains, there was no real threat to the medical post. And the war was coming to an end!

Instead of being forced to kill the enemy, Dad's job was to process our prisoners of war who had been shipped over from the Japanese prison camps. Many of the men were emaciated and ill, but with good medical care, most of them were soon ready to go home.

Home. To every one of those G.I.'s, home meant something different. To Corporal Holm, home was back in St. Paul Park, Minnesota, with Mom and the five-month-old son he had never seen. It was a joyous homecoming.

But being a practical man, Dad lost no time in getting back into the swing of civilian life. His old job at Sanitary Dairies was waiting for him. And, not wanting to impose on his in-laws any longer, he built a garage on a lot on Portland Avenue. Things were in short supply after the war and the Holms had neither a refrigerator nor indoor plumbing. They would come later.

When I came along on November 5, 1948, it was the converted garage at 932 Portland Avenue which I first learned to call home. There were only two or three other houses on our block. The rest was open, rolling fields covered by tall, coarse grass typical of the Mississippi Valley.

In the summertime, Doug and I spent a lot of time in those fields catching butterflies, snakes, and frogs. In the winter Mom bundled us up and

we rode our sleds down the snow-covered
street. Our only nearby playmates, Lila Has-
singer and Butch Hunter, usually tagged
along—ready for whatever sport Doug and I became engaged in.

I spent a lot of time at Grandma and Grandpa
Harbrecht's house on Third Street. He and my
grandmother were like a second set of parents to
me. Many a Saturday night found me curled up
on the floor watching wrestling matches on a
flickering black and white TV while Grandpa
nestled in his favorite rocker, an antique with
massive, carved arms.

A strong, powerfully-built man with straight,
thinning white hair, Grandpa Harbrecht was
something of an idol to me. I often wondered if
some of his endearing and unusual qualities
might have been handed down by his German
ancestors and, hopefully, some of them might
rub off on me.

He never owned an automobile and walked
everywhere. On his walks, he usually stopped
and chatted with somebody about the Lord.

There was never any question about Grandpa
Harbrecht's standing with the Lord. He and the
Almighty were on the best of terms, and it was
just natural that Grandpa should mention His
name frequently in conversations with other
friends.

And that's another thing Grandpa did well—
talk. He never met a stranger. The routine question "How are you feeling?" was always met
with a sprightly reply, "Just right!" As far as I
was concerned, that just about said it for
Grandpa Harbrecht—he was just right!

Each summer my parents and grandparents spent a week's vacation at Cedar Lake near Aitkin, Minnesota. It was the highlight of the year for me. We spent the entire week fishing, swimming, and enjoying the lush Minnesota lakes and woods. Besides Cedar Lake, my family traveled to various places around the Duluth area including Temperance State Park on the north shore where the Temperance River flows into the mammoth Lake Superior, the world's largest freshwater lake.

It was easy to understand why the state was named Minnesota, a Dakota Indian word meaning "sky-tinted water." Although there are more than 15,000 sky-blue lakes and rivers, the state is often called "the land of 10,000 lakes."

The scenic beauty, sparkling lakes, deep pine woods, and abundance of game fish always reminded me of Longfellow's poem, "The Song of Hiawatha." I heard it first in Miss Archer's sixth-grade class. Listening to her dramatic reading, I could just see the young Indian moving as quietly as a deer among the waterfalls that "flashed and gleamed" and rivers that rushed through "palisades of pine trees."

Grandpa Harbrecht had a natural love for the outdoors. Most of his free time was spent hunting, and ice fishing. The backs of his hands were lined and leathered like the skin on a snapping turtle's legs. One could easily see on Grandpa the mark of the rugged Minnesota weather.

Birthdays, weddings, anniversaries—as well as the normal run of holidays—were always family occasions around our house. That meant an influx of relatives from near and far. Two of

Mother's brothers, Clarence and Ray, lived nearby as did a sister, Lorena. Their youngest brother, John, had died at the age of sixteen in a tragic hunting accident.

Whenever we got together for family gatherings, Aunt Lorena could hardly wait to get in a word about *her* Jesus. Ultimately, she progressed to telling everybody about the Holy Spirit and speaking in tongues. The other family members had different church backgrounds, but they loved Aunt Lorena and "put up" with her "interpretation."

Our family abided by an unspoken code: "We may disagree among ourselves, but woe to the outsider who makes any disparaging remarks."

Uncle Ray, Mom's oldest brother, lived down on Grey Cloud Island, around which the backwaters of the Mississippi River swirled. I regularly walked through the woods to his house, stopping off to investigate "nature finds," or to spear carp in the bays and inlets of the Mississippi.

Some of my best memories are of the days spent at Uncle Ray's place—playing with his hunting dogs, fishing, canoeing, or helping him clear trees off his land.

During the winter, I ice fished and skated on the frozen waters of the Mississippi. At times when the ice hardened thick enough, Uncle Ray drove his jeep out onto the frozen surface and pulled Doug and me on snow skis.

Between my Uncle Ray and Uncle Kise, I would learn early a love and respect for nature that would grow stronger through the years.

It was Mother's second oldest brother who

was a particular favorite of mine. Although his given name was Clarence, everybody called him "Kise." There was a lot of my grandpa in Kise. He spent much of his time in the backwoods of Minnesota, too.

Uncle Kise and I developed an easy-going camaraderie. He recognized in me that same in-born love of the outdoors. Soon we were making frequent trips to the woods and lakes. With the help of my dad and Uncle Kise, I quickly learned the difference between a walleye, a northern, a crappie, and a bluegill.

There wasn't a lot of talking on these hunting and fishing trips. Strong and silent, Uncle Kise didn't waste words. Unless he had something on his mind, he just kept quiet. It is a trait that, some say, characterizes me.

When I was about twelve, Uncle Kise taught me how to shoot a .22 rifle. His instructions were simple and precise, "Lay the cross hairs of that sight on your target, relax, take a deep breath, and let it out easy."

I followed his instructions to a T and, each time I fired, a tin can fell.

"We've got a natural-born marksman here," Uncle Kise smiled, patting me on the back.

I swelled with pride. "Just like Grandpa."

3

AT MY WORST YOU FOUND ME

If I received my love of the outdoors from my mother's side of the family, I guess I got my musical heritage from my father's side. Music was a way of life to the Holms, who were raised Baptists. Most of Robert Holm's thirteen children played some kind of musical instrument. They were all self-taught musicians, including my dad, who played the guitar. I dearly loved the times when Dad got out his guitar and picked a few tunes. He and Mom occasionally sang in church.

St. Paul Park had only one grammar school, Oltman Elementary, a one-story, red-brick building, which was situated about a half mile from our house. The school had a good music program and Doug began taking trumpet lessons in the fourth grade. I must have been following in my big brother's footsteps when I started trombone lessons in the same grade. That was the year warm, grandmotherly Mrs. Boeck was my teacher.

A year or so later I started playing around with

an old guitar, an F-hole acoustic with metal strings, that belonged to Dad. I used to sit around in the basement plunking on the instrument. I didn't know the correct way to strum the thing, so I'd lay it down flat on my lap and press my thumbs on the strings to produce what sounded like chords.

Doug had become fairly proficient with the guitar. I tried to imitate every move he made. At times I'd watch musicians on television playing the guitar and then run for Dad's battered instrument to see if I could make my fingers chord as the "pros" were doing. My ear told me if it sounded right.

Doug was everything a big brother could possibly be. We ate, slept and played together. Some people didn't think we were normal because we didn't fight more. My continual teasing could have provoked fights, but Doug's elastic patience usually held out.

After he reached his teens, Doug began playing with various musical groups. By the time I hit junior high school, one of the groups, called "The Avantis," needed another guitar player. It was then I got my first taste of playing rock-and-roll music.

I had been aware of the rock sound for several years. Doug had bought an early Elvis Presley record, the large 78 rpm type, when we were first fooling around with Dad's guitar. I never forgot seeing Elvis on Ed Sullivan's show when the cameras could only show him from the waist up because of his notorious "swivel hips." The girls in the studio screamed wildly anyway, since they caught all the action live.

Pop music styles changed in late 1963 and early 1964 when the Beatles invaded the States from England. It was no longer the heyday of the single performer as in the late 50's with Elvis, Jerry Lee Lewis, Little Richard, and Buddy Holly. Elvis was making movies in Hollywood; Jerry Lee's career was in eclipse; Little Richard had a celebrated religious conversion; Buddy Holly was dead.

Folk music had enjoyed brief popularity, but the "group" sound was in vogue now with four guys harmonizing to an electrified rock beat. English groups like the Rolling Stones, the Who, the Animals, the Zombies, Herman's Hermits—all rode the top of the music charts.

When I got my teeth into that kind of music, I sat in school and daydreamed for hours about playing. Nothing else mattered. Getting together with several buddies, we formed "The Malibus" and began playing at the local dances and parties. I sang lead on most of the songs as well as playing lead guitar.

My parents always insisted that practice sessions for the band be held at our house. It was their subtle way of keeping tabs on things. They were both concerned about my playing in the rock group.

"We're not going to say you can't," Mom constantly told me, "but I hope someday you'll be so sold out to the Lord that playing in the band will not seem so important to you."

"Oh, Mom, come on," I pleaded, hoping to get her off my back. To myself I was thinking, *No way will I ever believe my playing rock music is not important*! Man, that's practically all I ever thought about.

But my mother had a way of gently getting her point across. I couldn't get away from her comments about the rock band. If it really bothered her that much, maybe I ought to think it over.

I knew I wasn't living up to the good example my parents had set for us kids—or even what I felt was right for myself. Once, when I was nine, I had asked Jesus into my heart. At the time I had really meant it. But as I grew older, other interests took priority. I was still attending Sunday School and church with the family, but my heart and my dreams were still all wrapped up in rock music.

There had been a few problems along the way that tended to confuse me. Mother and some of her friends had become interested in a deeper walk with the Lord. That led them on a concerted search of the Scriptures. They wound up receiving the gift of the Holy Spirit and the experience of speaking in tongues. That created problems in the traditional church we attended.

So, our family began visiting churches in the area looking for a new church home. My parents finally settled on the Summit Avenue Assembly of God in St. Paul. Doug and I were reluctant to switch churches, though. I just couldn't understand the need to change. After all, we had attended the other church all of my life. Mom and Dad had made their commitment to Christ in that church just before their marriage.

"We won't make you attend the new church," Mom suggested one day. "We'd like for you to visit and see how you like it, though."

Dad nodded. "That's right. If you aren't

happy there and can't find any friends your age, you can remain at the other church. Just give the new church a fair chance."

"Okay," I agreed reluctantly.

I planned on *not* liking the new church. I guess any teenager would resent being suddenly uprooted from familiar surroundings. Yet, the first Sunday we visited, I was impressed with the sanctuary—a handsome brick and wood structure with exposed beams. To my surprise, I also found a lot of kids who seemed to be enjoying themselves. Not only that, the church had a real orchestra.

"Hey, we've got a spot for you fellows any time you can make it," the director announced invitingly to Doug and me.

More than anything else, it was the music that won me over. When those people sang hymns—even the songs I'd heard all my life—it just wasn't like anything I'd ever felt before. There was a soul-stirring quality to their singing. And I liked it.

The fall of 1965 I entered my senior year at St. Paul Park High School. The Malibus had become more popular than ever. We were booked many weekends to play dances and parties. There were bigger, brighter opportunities on the horizon—talk of a record, touring as far east as Chicago. At the same time, oddly enough, I was growing disenchanted with the whole rock scene.

One of our dates that fall was the annual high school homecoming dance. The gym, decorated with brightly colored streamers, was dimly lit, and vibrated with the beat of our music. Everybody was dancing to the frenzied rhythm. The floor was a dizzying blur of kids caught up in the mindless mood we had created.

That night as I played my guitar and sang, I found myself taking a long, hard look around me. I was strangely detached from myself. I've heard of people who claim to have died, whose spirits move out of their bodies and observe everything from a distance. I think it was something like that.

Suddenly, I felt I was standing offstage, watching myself and my friends, the kids, the whole scene. And, for the first time, I saw things as they really were—phony.

As long as we had kept the beat going, nobody noticed the band as individuals. Just as we swung into a message song, some guy shouted, "Hey, can't you play something we can dance to?" The beat. That's all they cared about. Nobody was listening to the lyrics.

Anyway, the songs I was writing and singing—the ones about freedom and peace— seemed empty and hollow. I knew they lacked reality. I had tried to write songs with meaning and significance—songs that communicated something worthwhile. But all they cared about was the beat.

Following the dance that night, I left for a weekend retreat sponsored by our church. I don't know how I got roped into that, although most Christians in the church probably figured I was one of them. I was morally straight, came from a good Christian home, could use all the right words and phrases when I needed to. I was

Mr. Nice Guy. The same thing was true when I was with my worldly buddies. I could speak their language too—profanity and all. I was tough, cool. I was straddling the fence—trying to keep a toehold in both worlds—and faking it pretty good.

On the retreat, in the space of a few short hours, I was faced with a decision. The lines were clearly drawn. What would it be? The world of strobe lights and one-night stands or a total sell-out to the Lord? All weekend long the retreat speaker seemed to be speaking directly to me.

The retreat ended on Sunday, October 17, 1965. I'll never forget that day.

All of the kids went back to church that night for a youth service. Doug and I had been asked to play a special number—me on piano, which I had learned by this time, and he on trumpet.

Apparently, word had gotten around church that I was also playing in a rock band. Some of the church members had even been so bold as to discuss it with my parents, and several people had spoken to the pastor.

On this particular night, Pastor Richard Dresselhaus, a tall, friendly man, headed us off before the service began and escorted us into his office.

"Some of the folks have been concerned about you guys," he began cordially. "They have questioned how you can feel right about playing in both church and rock groups. Maybe it's worth thinking about. I just wondered how it is with you guys—are you living for the Lord?"

Doug looked at me and then back at the

pastor. "No problem here," he answered.

I knew that was true. Doug *had* spent some rough days after finishing high school in 1963. He dropped out of college after a year and traveled around the west on a motorcycle for a time. Then, while portraying the role of Christ in a passion play in Colorado, he had recommitted his life to the Savior. He had really gotten his act together.

"And what about *you*, Dallas?" the pastor asked, looking me in the eye.

"Well, there could be some improvements," I squirmed.

He smiled. "Even as Christians we all have some improvements to be made, but that's not what I'm really talking about."

Suddenly, I couldn't put it off any longer. Again I could see the whole shallow scene—all the time and energy I had spent in practice sessions and playing for dances and parties. What real difference had it made anyway? After the last dance, the last song—it was all over. All of that energy and excitement I had invested in rock music hadn't affected a single life. And that was important to me. I wanted to do something that counted.

Pastor Dresselhaus interrupted my reverie. "What I'm really asking is this—do you know the Lord?"

Tears sprang to my eyes. "No, not really," I stammered, as I cradled my head in my hands.

"Dallas, the Bible says if you confess your sins, God is faithful to forgive and cleanse you from all wrong," he said earnestly. "Isn't that what you really want?"

"Yes."

The word jumped out of my mouth before my mind could stop it. The significance of what I had just said began to take hold. I knew enough about spiritual things to know I was not just applying for membership in a club or even a local church. I was committing my very life to the God of this universe—the God who had given His only Son for me.

The thing that finally got to me more than anything else was the realization the Jesus suffered and died for me. I had heard that familiar story all my life and knew it was true. There was only one reason I hadn't accepted His love before now. It was simply this: *What will my friends think if I become a Christian?* Suddenly, I realized there wasn't a friend in the world who would ever love me like Jesus.

My thoughts were interrupted by the pastor's next words.

"Dallas, let's pray."

I followed along behind Pastor Dresselhaus, repeating the simple prayer as he prayed. "Dear Jesus—Forgive my sins—I'm sorry—Come into my life."

I savored those words with every bit of sincerity I could put into them. They tasted good.

Even as I spoke the words, I could sense a change taking place. I was aware of His presence. I felt His love. I knew I could never be the same.

When we finished, there really wasn't much left to say. I think we all knew the work had been done.

I remember after stepping out of the office, my

brother grabbed me by the shoulders, looked me in the eye, and asked, "Did you really mean what you said in there?"

Once again that word found its way from my heart to my lips. "Yes."

How could You love me, Jesus?
How did You know my name?
Why did You save me, Jesus?
Oh, I'll never know
How You loved me so.
And I'll never see
What You saw in me . . .
At my worst You loved me—
*And now I love you, too.**

Pastor Dresselhaus shook my hand. "You'll never regret this decision," he smiled. "This will be a day to remember."

Doug and I walked back upstairs for the service. "Before we play tonight, my brother has something he wants to say," Doug announced.

I saw my mother glance quickly at my dad when I stepped forward. The auditorium was hushed.

"I've talked to the pastor tonight," I said. "I guess I've been trying to ride the fence—play the world's kind of music and walk with the Lord. Tonight, I realized I can't do both. I have to choose. I've decided to give my talent to the Lord. From now on I'm committing myself totally to Jesus Christ."

"Amen!" several people chorused.

"Praise the Lord!" echoed some others.

Three rows back, I saw the tears glistening in my mother's eyes. I knew she had been praying long and hard that I would take this stand. Little did I know that she was now praying I would have the strength to keep the courage of my new-found convictions.

4

I'M TELLING THEM TODAY

Dobie Gray had a hit song that summer called "The In Crowd." While all the kids were humming it, dancing to its upbeat tempo, and flipping their radio dials to catch it on the local Top-40 station—I was *living* it!

More than anything else, I guess that was the reason I hadn't become a Christian any sooner. I was *in* with the in crowd. The lead singer of a popular rock group just naturally belonged to the in crowd at St. Paul Park High School.

The familiar rap against Christians was, "They're losers." There had to be something wrong with you if you were a Christian. Most non-believers considered them sub-human or "a couple of bricks shy of a full load."

And, of course, there was no other outlet for a guy with talent who'd suddenly dropped rock and roll. There were no Christian radio stations, and contemporary Christian music, as we know it now, didn't exist.

That night, after I made my public profession of faith at church, I went straight home to my room and closed the door. I needed time to think.

The streetlight was shining through the window that faced Portland Avenue, illuminating the entire room with a soft glow. I threw myself across the bed.

A little later I would realize that some things had changed instantly and drastically. For one thing, I would never again—even *once*—be tempted to use foul language. For another, the desire to return to the rock world *for any reason*—enjoyment, fame, money, popularity— was completely gone. It was a total, dramatic change. Before I became a Christian, actually only hours before, rock music was my life— absolutely everything I had ever wanted.

But even though the Lord had changed me on the *inside*, it was going to be up to me to deal with the *outside* circumstances that hadn't changed—like my friends.

I feared losing most of the friends I had known since grade school. I wasn't sure how to go about telling them what had happened to me— especially the Malibus. Besides, we had a couple of engagements coming up. What should I do about those?

I began to feel nervous and, quite frankly, a little scared. I thought to myself, *Do I have to go around telling everybody, or can I just live it and maybe they won't really catch on and give me a bad time?*

While I was wrestling with these questions, wondering what my next move should be, a knock came at my bedroom door.

"Who is it?" I called.

"It's me," my mom said. "I have something I'd like to share with you."

"Come on in, Mom."

Mother sat down on the edge of the bed as I flicked on the overhead light.

"I have something to read to you from the Bible," she said softly.

"Go ahead."

She opened her well-worn Bible to the twelfth chapter of Romans and read: "I urge you therefore, brethren, by the mercies of God, to present your bodies a living and holy sacrifice, acceptable to God, which is your spiritual service of worship. And do not be conformed to this world, but be transformed by the renewing of your mind, that you may prove what the will of God is, that which is good and acceptable and perfect" (1, 2, NASV).

"You couldn't have come at a better time," I said, feeling greatly relieved. "That Scripture answers a lot of questions for me. Thanks."

"Good. Now get some sleep," she smiled, leaning over to kiss me good night.

It was settled. I wouldn't wait. Tomorrow I would tell the guys in the rock band that I would no longer be part of that scene. God's Word had made it clear what my new life in Christ should be. The words of a song I later wrote expressed how I felt on my way to school the next day.

What am I gonna do?
What am I gonna say?
And how'm I gonna feel
If I tell them today?

That I'm just not the same,

I've had a change of heart.
Last night I met the Lord
And I found a brand-new start.

But will they understand
That I still like 'em so?
I do want them to stay
And I do want them to go;
I still want them around
But I want us apart,
I wanna keep right on,
But I've found a brand-new start.

How can they understand
What I am trying to say?
How can they realize
That I'm just not the same.

But, Lord, why should I care
After what You've done for me?
You broke those chains of sin
And you set me oh so free!
That's more than all my friends
Have ever done before,
That's why I'm gonna live
For You all the more.

I know now what I'll do
And I know what I'll say,
And I don't care how I feel—
I'm telling them today!*

The next day when the bell rang, signaling the end of my first-period class, I walked out the door and almost ran headlong into Don Moore, the drummer for our group.

"Say, Dallas, I'm glad I caught you," he

---

smiled. "I've scheduled some dates for later this month, and I want to check to see if you're free."

"Sorry, I'm not going to play with the group anymore," the words were out, almost before I had a chance to think about my reply.

"Oh, yeah, sure," he laughed.

"I'm serious, Don."

"Come on, Dallas. Quit kidding around. We've got to know about these dates," he repeated.

"But I won't be playing with you guys anymore."

We walked down the stairs, still talking. For some reason, he thought I was still kidding him and grew more and more upset. Finally, we reached the bottom of the stairs, unaware that we were blocking the stairway. Impatiently, the kids pushed past us.

"I just don't feel right about it anymore," I said.

"You're *really* serious?" he mumbled.

"Yeah, I'm really serious," I replied. "I think the One who gave me whatever talent I have wants me to use it for Him. Up to now I haven't used it that way. I think it's about time I started."

Don walked away shaking his head. The conversation was pretty much a carbon copy with each of the other guys in the group. Gary Hajek, the band's bass player, was the only one who accepted my decision gracefully. It just didn't seem to matter one way or the other to him.

The word spread fast around school. A few old friends noticed. "He's changed," they said. By their tone of voice, I was pretty sure they didn't mean it as a compliment. Others gave me the cold shoulder. One guy spent a lot of time making cracks like, "He's got religion," and calling me "Preacher Man."

As many of my old friends dropped away, I was left with a lot of free time on my hands. Invitations to sing and play for various church groups cropped up within a few weeks. An ex-rock-and-roll singer was a "trophy" to some people. They viewed me as one snatched right out of the clutches of the devil himself.

Churches called, asking me to speak to their young people. At first, I accepted most of the invitations. I felt like I had a message and kids my age were the ones who needed to hear it. That seemed the obvious thing to do until Pastor Dresselhaus gave me another point of view one day while we were chatting in his office.

"You may not understand this right now, but I want to give you some good advice," he offered. "It's the kind of advice some people who've just met the Lord don't care to hear—but I think you'll be grateful for it in time."

"What's that?"

"The best thing you can do right now—even in the face of all these invitations—is to restrict your speaking and singing to once a month."

"Once a month, huh?"

"That's right," he responded. "Primarily, you need to stick around the church and listen to what God is saying to His people. You've got some growing to do first—some seasoning. Read your Bible daily. Learn the ways of the Lord. Prepare yourself. If you do that, the day will come when you will be ready to serve God. And there will be a place for you. I guarantee that."

Pastor Dresselhaus and I were as different as two people could possibly be. I was an ex-rocker, "cool" in dress and speech. He was right off an Iowa farm, crewcut and conservative. Yet, I respected him, and, in spite of the fact that I was green in the things of the Lord, I knew exactly what he was saying. Prepare yourself, get some experience, and God will use you—in His own time.

Some things are worth waiting for.

5

WHEREVER HE LEADS

For six months or so I followed Pastor Dresselhaus' advice and accepted only a limited number of invitations to sing.

Then Phil Ekstedt, a talented musician and singer himself, invited me to sing with him at a couple of church gatherings. We had known each other ever since my family joined Summit Avenue Assembly of God church. He was one of the first of the new group of friends I made after becoming a Christian.

Phil had written a lot of songs that came across in a folk-like style when performed with guitars. We also did some traditional hymns jazzed up with our new arrangements.

At first, a lot of churches were skeptical of our brand of music. We didn't sing the typical Christian songs. Besides that, we played guitars—instruments some people considered "tools of the devil."

While some of the older members of the audiences reacted to our music with indifference, the young people always responded with warmth and enthusiasm.

One by one, the doors were opening. To my surprise and delight, I realized the Lord could use the talent I had all along. I could play my guitar and sing for Jesus. It seemed like a natural combination.

After several months, Phil began talking about having a record pressed so we could sustain our ministry.

"A record would at least buy a few hamburgers and a little gas," he suggested.

"Speaking of hamburgers," I grinned, rubbing my stomach.

"Enough said," Phil nodded.

Phil had a contact with a small recording station located at Radio Station KNOF in St. Paul. The place had a tape recorder and some ancient microphones set up in a studio the size of a postage stamp. For a few hundred dollars, we could get a couple of hundred albums.

He wrote several of the songs on the album and we cut these, along with three standard hymns with our "new" arrangements. We backed ourselves on guitars, with Don Moore, the drummer from my former rock group, on drums. The album was entitled simply: "Phil and Dallas Sing."

Phil, a second-year student at North Central Bible College in Minneapolis, was a prime influence in my decision to go there. Pastor Dresselhaus had suggested that I find a good Bible school. Since I planned to be involved in some kind of ministry, Bible college was obviously the best place to prepare myself.

In September of 1966, I enrolled at North Central. It was that fall Grandpa Harbrecht went home to be with the Lord.

I guess I thought Grandpa Harbrecht would always be around. He never complained and though I knew he was aging, the sparkle in his eye was that of a younger man. Since Grandma's death almost four years before, he had enjoyed staying with various relatives. He died unexpectedly one afternoon while sitting in a chair in Aunt Lorena's dining room.

She had just come into the room and asked, "And how are you feeling this morning, Dad?"

"Me? Why, I'm just right!" he replied. Then, he took a deep, sighing breath and died.

He was still seated in the chair, his body slumped slightly forward, his hands resting on his cane in a familiar pose when the other family members arrived.

He looked so alive sitting there that it was hard to believe his spirit had already gone to be with the Lord. And when the coroner was called to examine the body, he found, just as Grandpa had always predicted, that the swollen, discolored, pain-filled legs were perfectly normal! God had, indeed, answered his prayer. Except for the tired old heart that had just decided to stop beating, he was in perfect physical condition!

For days I struggled over Grandpa's death. We had been so close over the years, I felt as if I had lost one of my parents. I vowed to the Lord that I'd try to be the kind of Christian man Grandpa had been. It would take some doing. Grandpa had left some pretty big shoes for a grandson to fill.

The first half of the year at North Central, Phil and I roomed together, traveled together, and went to classes together. That was a lot of togetherness. I honestly think we wore out the friendship. The decision to go our separate ways for the rest of the year was mutual. Each of us had some other ideas we wanted to explore—musically.

Music was the most important thing in my life—besides the Lord. One day in Bible class, that focus became apparent to a number of people.

"When you graduate from school, what do you plan on doing with your life?" asked Brother Phillips.

One senior raised his hand. "Well, bless God!" he responded enthusiastically. "I'm going to do whatever the Lord wants me to do. I just want to be obedient to Him. I may be a missionary. I may be a pastor. I'm not sure yet, but whatever—I'm following Him."

The class members nodded approvingly when he finished. A few applauded.

Another fellow raised his hand with basically the same statement. "I don't have any job offers at this point," he said, "but I want to follow the Lord's leading."

Still another student raised his hand and stated a similar purpose. It seemed most of the guys had one thing in mind—doing whatever the Lord wanted. But nobody had anything specific in mind.

Finally, I raised my hand.

"Okay, Dallas," the teacher said, pointing to me.

I cleared my throat as I stood. "I want to sing to thousands of people. I want to make records. I want to be on radio and television and reach as many people as I can for the Lord."

Some of the people in the class turned and looked at me strangely. They obviously thought I had a giant ego problem. That wasn't the case at all. I simply knew *what* I was equipped to do and was preparing to do it with all diligence.

As I applied that approach to my life, it took me into some unusual places—seedy jails, tiny storefront churches, and depressing rest homes. Most of the time I was not paid, but I wasn't there for the money. I was there to please the God who had called me out of darkness. That was reward enough.

Living in the dormitory through the week, I rode my motorcycle home on the weekend to spend time with my parents. Dad had a Volkswagen bus which he used for transportation to work. Each Friday he washed the bus and filled the tank with gas. I used it on the weekends I had opportunities to minister.

"It'd be kinda nice not to have the bus brought back with an empty tank for a change," Dad remarked wistfully one day.

"I'm sorry, Dad. I'll be glad when we're earning enough to pay you back. Right now, though, most of the folks don't have anything, and when they do take up an offering, it's only a few dollars.

Dad shrugged his shoulders and smiled, "In that case don't worry about it. Just consider that my donation to the cause."

"Thanks, Dad," I grinned.

Several times I was invited to a local church like the Minneapolis Evangelistic Auditorium when a revival was in progress. After my first revival, the evangelist, a short man with an electric grin and thick, wavy hair, was very complimentary.

"Man, that's really great singing," he said. "I'd like to have you for a meeting with me in Florida."

"Great!" I responded.

"I'll be in touch," he promised.

I got all excited about that invitation and waited impatiently to hear from the evangelist. But the days drifted into months. Eventually, I realized the preacher wasn't going to follow through. The experience was temporarily deflating.

That wasn't the end. The very same thing happened three more times in succession. I knew one day I'd be promoted from singing in rest homes, storefront chapels, and jails. Not that I minded. But I was developing a burden for reaching out in other areas, too.

Finally, I just left it with the Lord. "Father, I know it's not any individual who will make this ministry suceed. It's You—in Your timing and on Your terms. I'm here only to please You."

Another lesson learned. People can be fickle. Crowds can make or break their idols. Besides, I wasn't anybody special—just another singer, singing His songs. When He needed me elsewhere, He'd let me know. Meanwhile, I'd bide my time.

During my sophomore year at North Central, I got a janitorial job with the Billy Graham Association in Minneapolis.

The only singing I did there was while I was cleaning out the restrooms or mopping the cafeteria floor. I started working in the Decision building, where they mailed out the *Decision* magazine. Later on, I was promoted up to the main building where the real heart of the organization functioned. There, I worked in the stockroom, keeping inventory, filling requisitions, and loading and unloading trucks.

On Wednesdays, we usually had a chapel service. One time Billy Graham himself spoke to us and after the service, many crowded around to meet him. I've always respected Dr. Graham as a great man of God. I would have liked to have met him that day but I guess I was never too good at taking the initiative of introducing myself to people. Besides, I figured a busy man like Dr. Graham probably wouldn't be too excited about meeting a stockboy. Well, maybe someday . . .

By this time, I had experimented with writing some songs trying to explain—even though feebly at times—the great joy of knowing and serving Jesus Christ. "I Saw The Light" was one of the first I wrote with this message.

I was sinking deep in sin,
Had no peace or joy within,
Then I, then I saw the Light!

I knew God could put me right,
but I kept wand'ring day and night,
'Til I, 'til I saw the Light.

I tho't I was having fun,

When my life was on the run;
God came down and changed my ways,
Turned my darkest nights to days!

I'm no longer deep in sin,
I've got peace and joy within;
Now I, now I see the Light.

The second verse was aimed at the listeners. I didn't want to miss a chance to cause them to do some thinking for themselves—a chance to make a life-changing decision.

Do you live in untold sin?
Do you have a peace within?
Do you, do you see the Light?

Do you think you're having fun,
When your life is on the run?
Jesus Christ can change your ways,
Turn your darkest nights to days!

Then you'll live no more in sin,
You'll have peace and joy within
*When you, when you see the Light!**

The big thing in Bible college was finding the will of God for your life. One could easily get the impression from listening to some that God's will was a dark, mysterious thing that He might share with you if you were in the right place at the right time. Or it was like looking for a needle in a haystack. There also seemed to be an element of fear involved. Some suggested He might even go so far as to call you to a job you wouldn't

---

be able to handle or send you away from family and friends to some heathen country—like Africa.

I guess some of those impressions must have been on my mind the night I went to chapel and saw a film on the life of missionary J.W. Tucker who was martyred in the Congo in 1964. I sat in the darkened chapel, gripped by the reality of a twentiety-century man who had actually laid down his life for the Lord.

Tucker had served as a missionary for more than twenty years when independence came to the former Belgian Congo. Violent fighting broke out among various factions. There was much bloodshed. Tucker and his family left the country in 1963. He didn't have to go back but, feeling the call of God, he returned to the country he had loved and served, only to be killed shortly afterward.

With the missionary's death, the thought struck me: the Lord needed someone to take his place. Who would He send? It would have to be someone dedicated to obeying God—someone willing to go anywhere—even Africa.

Suddenly, I felt the sweat breaking out on my forehead. My hands were cold and clammy. *Could that person be me?*

I was so involved with my music, I wondered how the Lord could possibly use me in the jungles. But the film clearly showed the need there. The Lord must have wanted me to see it. Was He speaking to me through the film? Somehow I didn't think strumming my guitar and singing "I Saw the Light" while wandering through the jungles of the Dark Continent was going to be all that successful. Back and forth I wrestled with the conflicting thoughts.

When the film ended, the chapel emptied quickly, students rushing to the student center for a late snack or to hit the books for tomorrow's classes. I was alone. A few lights cast a subdued glow over the room. I sat motionless, stunned by the impact of what I had seen and felt.

The words of an Ira Stanphill song came to mind:

No greater love hath mortal man
Than for a friend to die.*

I sensed that the Lord was wanting a commitment out of me greater than anything I had ever anticipated. Then I spoke aloud, breaking the silence.

"Lord, whatever You want, I'll do it. I know in my heart, I'll never be the happiest unless I'm doing what You want me to do. If you want me to go to Africa and be a missionary like J.W. Tucker, I'll go. If necessary, I'll forget all my own plans and schemes. Simply tell me what You want me to do."

Even as the words left my mouth, I felt peace descending upon me as I released the matter to the Lord. I could practically hear the Lord laughing as he tenderly spoke to me:

"I don't want you to go to Africa and be a missionary, Dallas. I haven't equipped you for that kind of job. I just want you to be willing to

---

go wherever I may call. That's all I desire from my followers."

He wasn't asking me to do something contrary to my nature and abilities. All He wanted was my unconditional surrender. The choice of how to best serve Him seemed to be mine. What pleased me most was doing His will. If it meant music or martyrdom—I was ready.

I walked out of the chapel that night feeling like a new man. I knew something significant had happened. I could never be the same again.

The moon hung full in the night sky. I wondered if it was symbolic. Somehow, I felt it was.

6

NO BETTER MODEL

The summer of 1968, between my sophomore and junior years in Bible college, I served as youth pastor at John Wilkerson's church in Kenosha, Wisconsin. It was my first experience in planning programs. Being something of a procrastinator, I have always been a shade un-disciplined in some areas. Now that I was responsible for leading other people, I was forced to organize my time more wisely.

Part of my responsibility included a Saturday night youth rally at an old theater in downtown Kenosha. I had a chance to sing before some large non-Christian crowds—my first real taste of front-line evangelism. I liked it.

That summer was a chaotic time for the country. President Johnson had decided not to run for re-election because of the war in Viet Nam. Both Martin Luther King and Robert F. Kennedy had been assassinated. The drug revolution was just beginning. Protest against the Viet Nam war was growing. It was a time of turmoil for many young people—some of whom would ultimately spill their blood in the steamy jungles of Southeast Asia. Many of those kids were searching for answers which I knew Jesus could give them.

Returning to school for my junior year, I formed a gospel trio with Sam Benson and Nancy Sirvio. After appearing in a number of churches, we decided to make a record. Borrowing a couple thousand dollars from my parents for the album, we went down to United Audio Studios in Minneapolis to record an album "I Saw The Light."

It was during my junior year that I became aware of a change in my mother. Many weekends when I came home from school, she would be in bed.

"Is anything wrong with Mother?" I asked my dad.

"She's just having a rough day," he replied, a worried look creasing his face.

That scene was repeated many weeks in a row. I had always known my mother as a witty, energetic person. Now she spent most of her time in bed, seemingly drained of strength and vitality. I knew something was seriously wrong.

For some time I felt guilty about Mother's condition. She had given so much to my brother, Doug, and myself. Now he was off in the Navy and I was away at school. I wondered if that had contributed to her depression. The doctors offered the usual "change of life" diagnosis, but there seemed to be more to Mother's problem than that.

Near the end of the school year, I came home one day to find Mother in bed as usual. Puffy, dark circles ringed her eyes; deep lines were etched in her face. She seemed worse than ever. Dad was sitting near the bed, with his head in his hands.

"Dallas, could you pray for your mother?" he asked softly.

I looked down at Mother and then over at Dad. I hurt so badly for them, my heart felt as if it was being crushed. Tears filled my eyes and ran down my face as I got down on my knees beside the bed and poured my heart out to the Lord.

When I stood up, Mother had tears in her eyes. So did Dad. "Dallas, hug your father," she said tearfully.

That was just something we never did. Doug, Dad, and I seemed to have a mutual, manly understanding that hugging was for women and little kids. We had left that behind—along with other symbols of our childhood. Nowadays, we shook hands—like men.

But that afternoon, as Dad and I reached for each other, the dam broke, crumbling all the barriers that men sometimes put up to protect their masculinity. A flood of tears left us feeling clean and new.

The experience ultimately changed all three of us—Mother, Dad, and me. I still don't understand why Mother had to be sick for so long. I do know that, in dealing with her physical and emotional problems, we learned compassion and understanding for other people. And we learned that some of the best communicating between parents and their grown-up children is done without words!

I received word soon after that experience that Pastor Ira Stanphill from the Rosen Heights Assembly of God church in Fort Worth, Texas, was looking for a youth pastor. John Wilkerson, Pastor Stanphill's brother-in-law, had recommended me for the job.

The school also gave me a good recommendation and, with the bonus of my musical background, I was hired. When the school session ended in May 1969, I moved to Fort Worth to assume the new position.

Pastor Stanphill, a practical, down-to-earth man with a great sense of humor, was an excellent preacher. He was also a well-known gospel songwriter. Some of his songs—such as "Room at the Cross for You," "Mansion Over the Hilltop," "Suppertime," and "Happiness Is"—have been sung and recorded by many singers and gospel groups.

Every couple of months at the church we had a special Sunday service in which he simply sat down at the piano and played some of his songs—both old and new. It was always a unique time at Rosen Heights.

Pastor Stanphill was a great encouragement to a budding songwriter like myself. "Keep your songs simple," he advised. "Don't write complicated things that people can't understand. Be plain. That's the way Jesus did it. There's no better model."

In retrospect, I would come to look back on those days in Fort Worth as some of the best in my life. Between being exposed to such a man of God like Ira Stanphill and working with a dedicated youth group, it was a time to remember.

7

OUR TIME HAS COME

I never thought much would come of the album, "I Saw the Light." Naturally, I sold a few copies to my family and friends, and a few more to the people who came to hear me sing. But that was about the extent of it.

Seven months after I moved to Fort Worth, the phone rang one night at my apartment.

"This is David Wilkerson," came a vibrant voice over the telephone. "I'm calling from Eugene, Oregon, where I'm holding a crusade. A friend of yours gave me an album you recorded. Good stuff! I've been looking for a singer to work with me in crusades. I think you may be my man."

The name, David Wilkerson, was certainly familiar to me and thousands of others all across the country. I knew Wilkerson as the founder of Teen Challenge and author of a best-seller turned movie, *The Cross and the Switchblade.*

Back in 1964, as a junior in high school, I had attended one of his meetings at Summit Avenue Assembly of God in St. Paul. But at the time I wasn't ready for anything the fiery evangelist had to offer. As I remember, I had sat in the back of the auditorium, clowning around with some of my pals, and successfully tuning him out.

"We'll be in Dallas for a crusade in about a month," he continued. "How about coming over and singing at the meeting? Afterwards, we could get together and talk."

I almost turned him down. I was happy in Fort Worth. Working with Brother Stanphill had been a joy. Yet, to my surprise, I heard myself accepting his invitation. "Sure. I'll be glad to."

I was well-prepared for disappointment. After all, I had received other offers that never panned out. So, this telephone call didn't excite me at first.

Then, as I hung up and began reflecting on our conversation, I sensed something different about the call. In fact, as the Spirit began to confirm the significance of my invitation, I picked up the phone again and dialed my fiancée, Linda Satterberg, in St. Paul.

We had been sweethearts since our high school days. Though I had been out with other girls occasionally, I had always known Linda was that special someone. Waiting for her to answer the phone, I did some reminiscing . . .

Interestingly enough, Dad met Linda long before I did. Growing up on Argyle Street in St. Paul, she lived a few doors down from the corner grocery where Dad delivered milk. The knobby-kneed, nine-year-old girl, her short curls bouncing, usually managed to make it to the store on errands for her mother just about the time Dad was making his daily delivery.

Linda liked the friendly milkman who always took time to notice her and speak to her. With green eyes wide, she would watch until he had deposited the last bottle in the dairy case. Then she would wave shyly and flit away.

Dad watched her blossom from a quiet, but inquisitive child into the pretty, poised young woman who greeted him in the lobby of Summit Avenue Assembly of God one Sunday soon after our family started attending services.

"Well, hello, Mr. Holm!" she exclaimed in delight. "What are *you* doing here?"

They agreed it was strange that they should have run into each other somewhere other than the dairy counter of the grocery store. Dad learned that Linda was almost a life-long member of the church, since she had committed her life to the Lord at the age of seven.

Dad had the jump on me, but it didn't take me long to notice the grown-up Linda! She was always in the thick of the youth activities at Summit Avenue. And, when Dale Tollefson came on the scene as youth director, the action picked up. Nearly every weekend he planned a hayride, picnic, or retreat where the kids could get together for some good, clean fun.

It wasn't until the night of the Halloween party, though, that I worked up the nerve to get better acquainted with Linda. The basement of the church had been mysteriously transformed with black crepe paper and jack-o-lanterns into the semblance of a haunted house. There was all the usual—lots of good food, plenty of cold drinks and punch, and those dumb party games.

Everyone came in costume. I finally spotted Linda and a girlfriend of hers dressed as Raggedy Ann and Raggedy Andy. The red rag-mop covering her dark hair almost threw me, but there was no mistaking those green eyes or that smile.

"Hey, Linda!" I called. "Is that really you?"

She laughed. "It's me, all right. But you're not supposed to be able to guess."

A buddy and I convinced the girls that the four of us would have a much better time upstairs. So we sneaked away from the party and spent the next hour in an empty Sunday School room around the piano, singing and talking.

From then on, I was hooked—on a little doll with two bright red spots on her cheeks and stars in her eyes. . .

Her soft voice on the other end of the line jarred my wandering thoughts.

"Hello?"

"Linda, guess who just called?"

"I give up. Who?"

"David Wilkerson!"

"David Wilkerson?! Isn't he that preacher who works with drug addicts in New York City or somewhere?"

"He's the one. But he also conducts evangelistic crusades all over the country. He's been looking for a singer. He heard the record we cut while I was at North Central and wants me to sing at a crusade in Dallas. If he likes me, the next stop is New York City!"

"Oh . . . that's really great." She sounded a little puzzled.

"What's wrong?"

"I think it's fine for *you*, but what about *us*?"

"What do you mean—for *me*? That doesn't change any of our plans. The wedding is still on."

"Oh!" She laughed, relieved. "I'm glad to hear *that*. For a minute I thought . . ."

Linda needn't have worried. The two of us were a team long before I heard from David Wilkerson.

On the night I was to sing for the crusade, I sat nervously in the pastor's study waiting to meet the world-famous evangelist. From the sanctuary of Oak Cliff Assembly of God, I could hear the buzz of the crowd.

"Looks like a packed house," someone said. "There must be at least two thousand people here tonight."

That information didn't do much to settle the butterflies in my stomach!

Two men entered the office briskly. Overhearing the introductions to some of the others in the room, I learned that the thin, intense man was David Wilkerson. He was closely followed by David Patterson, his crusade director.

"I'm Dallas Holm," I said to Brother Dave, extending my hand.

He grasped it and spoke cordially enough, but he seemed preoccupied and moved on quickly to speak to some other people. I was a little disappointed. After all, I was here because he had invited me. Actually, this was to be my "audition" as crusade soloist. He certainly didn't seem as enthusiastic as he had sounded on the phone.

But I was sure the meeting was weighing heavy on his mind.

A rousing chorus from the choir signaled that it was time for the service to begin. I took a deep breath and stepped out onto the platform behind Brother Dave and David Patterson.

I had sat on the platform at Rosen Heights church every Sunday. But facing the crowd in this jam-packed auditorium was not at all the same. In the audience I spotted a few familiar faces—some of the kids from my youth group. They grinned from ear to ear when they recognized their youth pastor and friend, sitting next to none other than David Wilkerson himself.

I'm sure the preliminaries took only minutes, but it seemed like hours. I was actually rather startled to hear the announcement that Dallas Holm would come to bring the special music.

I was so nervous I was sure I would forget the words or a guitar string would break. But as I began to play and sing, I felt that same peace flood over me and the entire audience that I had felt so often before. As I sang, I forgot all about my anxiety and even the fact that this was an audition of sorts. I was aware only that I was singing to the Lord and to the people He loved.

After I had finished my song and had taken my seat, Brother Dave came to the microphone. My first impression when I had met the thin, almost frail man was, *Could this really be the man who walked the streets of New York City alone, telling young killers about the love of Jesus?*

As he paced the platform, speaking with great forcefulness and intensity, I realized he *was* that man—and a whole lot more.

After the service, I drove Brother Dave back to the hotel. I was naturally curious about his reaction to my singing. His first remark came out of left field.

"I can't believe how quiet the audience was while you sang," he observed.

"Oh, that," I shrugged. "I've noticed it before. What's so special about that?"

"Well," he smiled, "it's pretty rare to find a singer who can command that kind of attention from an audience. Not all musicians or even preachers have that ability."

We finished the short drive in silence. I spent the time trying to digest all the impressions and feelings I had just experienced and, above everything else, to discern the leading of the Lord in it all.

David Patterson joined us in the coffee shop at the hotel. Brother Dave got right to the point.

"Dallas, what did you think of the service?"

"I've never seen anything like it," I shook my head in amazement. "There must have been two or three hundred people who came forward after the service."

"That's not at all unusual." He spoke without a trace of arrogance in his voice. "That's just the way the Lord does things in this ministry. Night after night, large numbers of people are saved or come forward to recommit their lives."

"There's no question that God is moving in your ministry." I was genuinely overwhelmed.

"How would you feel about working with us?" Brother Dave leaned back in his chair, studying my face intently.

I paused to get my thoughts together. I've

never been much of a talker and this was probably the most important speech I would ever make.

"I think this is what I've been waiting for ever since I became a Christian." The words came slowly and deliberately. "Only God could have brought about the things I've seen tonight. I think He has been preparing me for this kind of ministry all along."

Suddenly the prophetic words of Pastor Dresselhaus echoed in my memory. *Prepare yourself. Get some experience. And God will use you—in His own time.* It seemed His time had come.

"There is one other thing," Brother Dave was saying. "It's a question I ask everybody who joins our team. After this, I'll never ask it again."

From the tone of his voice, I expected some serious theological question requiring a few minutes in a soundproof booth. "Go ahead," I said.

"Do you have a daily devotional time with the Lord?" he asked.

"Yeah," I replied, slightly surprised by the question. "Yes, I do."

"Good!" he responded with an emphatic whack of his hand on the table. "That's all I wanted to know. That's the single most important element in this ministry. If I know you're keeping that relationship right, and that you're where you ought to be with the Lord, you'll never have any problems with me. You can count on me never to bring up the subject again. I'll just assume you're taking care of that matter."

David Patterson, the tall, blonde crusade director, had been sitting quietly throughout the conversation. Now he exchanged a knowing glance with Brother Dave. "I think he's the man," Patterson said.

He nodded, a wide grin breaking across his finely chiseled features. He thrust out his hand and shook mine.

"Welcome, Dallas. It's good to have you on the team. The people loved your music tonight. More importantly, they were moved by it. You'll be a real asset to the team."

The mood shifted noticeably. We could all feel the tension lift.

As the waitress refilled our coffee cups, the conversation took a different turn.

"Hey, Dallas, there's one question I didn't ask. How about your family? Is there a Mrs. Holm?"

"Not yet," I grinned, "but there soon will be. I'm getting married the last of December."

"We'll be needing you in New York by the first of the year. How does that fit into your plans?"

"Just right," I replied. "The wedding is December 27th. We'll drive out afterwards."

Linda Satterburg and I were married on a crisp cold Saturday night at the Summit Avenue church. In keeping with the event, a soft snowfall had frosted the trees and shrubbery like elaborate wedding cakes.

Inside, the flickering candles cast delicate shadows on the wall, illuminating the sanctuary filled with good friends and family members. Linda had known her maid of honor, Janice Ornburg, through most of her school years. And my brother, Doug, was my best man. Other lifelong friends completed the wedding party. They looked a little strange and stiff in their wedding finery—the guys in formal tuxedos and the girls wearing blue dresses, carrying small white fur muffs.

For just a minute, as I tugged at the collar of my rented tux, I wished I were somewhere fishing! That is, until I caught a glimpse of the beautiful girl in white walking down the aisle toward me. I don't remember much of what happened after that . . . except for the pastor's prayer.

Pastor Dresselhaus . . . the man who had led me to the Lord and had been so instrumental in those early years of my Christian walk. After the ceremony, Linda and I knelt before him as he laid hands on our heads, consecrating our lives and our marriage to God. He prayed with such fervor and compassion that there were few dry eyes in the building—including my own.

Then, as I played my guitar, Linda and I stood, facing each other, and sang a song I had written especially for the occasion—"Our Time Has Come." The time was here—a time of beginnings and endings, a time for seeking and finding, a time for following the Lord wherever He would lead for the rest of our lives.

Our time has come when we'll be one,
Joined here together on this day;
Joining our hearts, making a start
With what we have, we'll find a way.

We don't have much in the way of possessions,
But we've got each other and each other's affections.
The things of this earth seem to lose all their worth
When I'm near to you.

Side by side we will abide,
Pledging our love to one another.
Hand in hand, as one we stand,
Giving ourselves to each other.

---

* From "Our Time Has Come" by Dallas Hoam

8

688 BROADWAY

Linda and I stayed in St. Paul over the weekend. By Monday the weather had cleared enough to load my bronze and black Barracuda and the U-Haul trailer for the move to New York City. We were really packed tight—wedding presents, clothing, blankets—all our earthly possessions. At noon, we pulled out—bound for our new life with David Wilkerson and Teen Challenge. It would prove to be a genuine challenge before I was ever to sing my first song in a Wilkerson crusade.

From Minnesota eastward, the weather turned rough, with sleet and snow all the way. The Pennsylvania Turnpike was literally chewed up with potholes, the car and trailer catching every rut in the road.

Since Brother Dave would be out of town when we arrived, he had given me directions for locating our apartment—688 Broadway, Massapequa Park. In the excitement, I forgot all about the second half of the address. Besides, New York City is a pretty big place. There are highways and freeways and expressways and every-which-ways!

From the New Jersey side of the Hudson River, I crossed the George Washington Bridge and turned onto the Riverside Expressway which leads into Manhattan. When we came to a street marked "Broadway," I just naturally followed it, indirectly winding up in Harlem. Immediately, I sensed this was not the right spot for a white boy with Texas license plates on his car!

Past busy Times Square, I continued driving until I found the 600 block of Broadway. By this time, the elegant, high-rise district had given way to bleak-looking brownstones and faded, old tenements. Many were vacant and boarded up. Others looked like they had been gutted by fire. Garbage was strewn along the street, and drunks and winos lay in the gutter, wallowing in their own filth. All of which led me to believe we were in the right neighborhood. If this was not Skid Row, it was certainly right next door!

When we accepted Brother Dave's invitation, we didn't expect to find any stars in the part of Broadway where we were headed. We felt these were our people—the drunks, the kids on dope, the black leather jacket gangs. When Brother Dave had mentioned crusades, I saw myself singing to a bunch of down-and outers on some city street corner. But living right in the middle of the action appeared to be downright dangerous. Now that we were here, we'd just have to make the best of it.

Though I couldn't find a street number, I pulled up in front of a likely-looking spot, judging from the numbers on the adjoining buildings. It was a seedy, run-down tenement—pitch black inside with no sign of life. Linda and I just looked at each other. Neither of us said a word. But the question hung suspended between us—*Is this it?*

Hoping to find a number somewhere, I drove around the block once more and pulled in front again.

"Linda," I frowned, "I'm not sure this is the place. Let's pray about it."

"Let's do!" she agreed quickly.

"Lord," I prayed, "we've come this far by Your grace. You've brought us here to be involved in this ministry. We're here for that reason alone—to please You. If this is our new home, we accept it, knowing that You'll protect Linda when I have to be away. Lord, our lives belong to You. As long as You're with us, we have nothing to fear."

I decided to drive around the block one more time. I hadn't been able to find the correct driving lane all day. Horns blared constantly. Cars whizzed past. Cab drivers hollered, "Hey, cowboy, go park that horse!" It was all very bewildering.

We had been lost for over five hours. Linda looked worried and frightened. Under the circumstances, I wasn't feeling exactly comfortable myself. We had been driving all day in strange territory, pulling a heavy load. For a guy accustomed to the wide open spaces, the towering skyscrapers began to close in with the darkness. The noisy city sounds were a far cry from the soothing sounds of nature.

At the next stoplight, a taxi rolled up alongside. Hurriedly, I rolled down my window.

"Can you tell me where I can find 688 Broadway?" I asked.

"Broadway in Manhattan or Broadway out on Long Island?" he barked.

Then it clicked. I pulled the piece of paper from my pocket. "It says 688 Broadway, Massapequa Park."

"That's Long Island," said the cabbie. "Fella, you're at least sixty miles away!"

"How do I get there?"

"No problem, son." I think he had gotten a glimpse of Linda's stricken face and had softened up. "Just get back on Interstate 495. That'll take you to the Long Island Expressway. Head east until you come to Oyster Bay Expressway. Then turn right and go south. You can't miss it."

I thanked the cab driver and pulled up onto I-495. As I did, I noticed that the car was making a slight rocking motion. A quick look in the rearview mirror brought me to a complete stop. Sparks were flying like the Fourth of July!

When I got out to survey the damage, I saw that the heavy, overloaded trailer had pulled the bumper out of the back of the car. Only two safety belts had kept the trailer from being severed completely.

Thank You, Jesus! I murmured.

A few hundred yards away, I spotted a service station. Maybe if I crept along the access road, I could park at the station for the rest of the night. But that raised another question. Should we leave the trailer overnight with everything we owned inside?

We had been warned before we left Minnesota never to leave anything of value anywhere, unattended. "They'll rob you blind in New York City!"

Unfortunately, I didn't have any choice. The service station attendant let us park the trailer. It was now almost midnight. I was tired and weary from the long drive and the frustration of being lost in a big city. Linda was practically asleep already.

But our troubles were not over yet. As soon as I unhitched the trailer, the headlights on the car stopped working. That cost us another hour of wrestling in the dark with loose wires—some of which were live.

It was two o'clock in the morning before we finally located 688 Broadway in Massapequa Park. Naturally, the apartment manager had to be roused out of a sound sleep. Then we discovered the apartment was unfurnished. Another hour passed before we found a motel and fell into an exhausted sleep.

Everything had gone wrong. The whole trip had been a total disaster. If I ever had doubts about entering this ministry, it would have had to be at 2 A.M. on January 1, 1970. But Linda and I were still committed to the idea.

Sometimes, as I reflect back on our shaky beginnings, I have to believe that God allowed all those things to happen to test our motives. If we weren't thoroughly discouraged by now, He must have figured we had the intestinal fortitude it would take to do the job He had for us!

A couple of days later, Brother Dave was back in town. We met his wife, Gwen, along with David Patterson's wife, Carol, and the others who worked in the New York offices.

The apartment at 688 Broadway looked pretty good to us after the tenement down in the Bowery. But after we had settled in, we realized it wasn't the Waldorf, either. There was a leak in the bathroom, and every time it rained, the bathroom flooded. We had no furnishings except for a hideaway bed the Pattersons had left. A small scatter rug or two was our only floor covering, and there were no curtains for the windows—hardly an ideal first home.

Before Linda had a chance to fix things up in the apartment, she became very ill and we got another taste of life in the big, impersonal city. The hospital where I rushed her was noisy and overcrowded. Since there was not a room available when we checked in, she was stuck in a drafty hallway, shielded from passersby by only a heavy, white curtain.

I was more than a little scared. Married less than two weeks, fifteen hundred miles from home, my new bride ill. With the exception of the Teen Challenge family, we didn't know a single soul among the eight million people living in New York City. It seemed the tests of our faith were coming thick and fast.

Two days later, following a series of tests and X-rays, Linda was dismissed from the hospital. But the doctors still hadn't been able to come up with a diagnosis for the large amounts of blood she had been passing. After a brief stay in bed, the mysterious problem vanished as quickly as it had appeared, and Linda devoted her time to helping out in the crusade office and in trying to make the apartment more pleasant and livable.

My first trip as part of the crusade team was to Mobile, Alabama. That first night I was a little concerned. I knew the crowds would be two or three thousand strong with a good sprinkling of street kids. I wondered if it was possible to walk out there with my guitar and a ninety percent or better chance of a poor PA system, and command their attention with Christian songs.

But the same attentiveness Brother Dave had mentioned before gripped the crowd in Mobile. As I shared and sang, there was total silence—no heckling, no noise or commotion of any kind. The Lord was there that night and every night after that.

While standing backstage with Brother Dave in the "Afterglow" service, he motioned to me. "Dallas, I want you to talk with that nice-looking young fellow who came forward tonight. Find out his needs. Pray with him."

As other counselors paired off with inquirers, I walked over and introduced myself to the tall, well-groomed man Brother Dave had pointed out. The man told me that he was an actor who had played a role in the movie "2001." He had traveled all over the world, had had his share of beautiful women, and lived a glamorous lifestyle. But he had burned out on the world, and now he was giving his life to Christ.

"You might be interested to know it was your sharing plus your songs that got through to me," he told me.

I was to hear that same testimony in crusade after crusade. Under Brother Dave's preaching, thousands were being won to Christ. And many others who were not reached by his preaching were somehow claimed through my songs. I was realizing the fulfillment of my desires ever since college days—that of reaching as many people as possible with the message of the Gospel. I was grateful to Brother Dave for encouraging me and giving me an opportunity to get closer to the people. It wasn't enough to sing from a platform. I wanted to get down where the people were—to deal with their hurts and needs.

Between tours, when we were in town, we held street meetings in the inner city—Harlem, Greenwich Village, East Village. One of the most popular hangouts for the hippie crowd was The Electric Circus. Later, that nightspot would be bombed out by a radical group. We'd drop in from time to time just to see what was going on and if we could help. I got to know the kind of kids Brother Dave writes about in *The Cross and the Switchblade*—spaced out, hung over, the smell of pot everywhere. These were society's hardcore dropouts.

Jesus died for these people. And I cared about them. But, as time passed, I began to feel an even greater burden for kids a lot like I had been—basically pretty decent kids who went to church, or at least knew what was right. I wanted to tell them that in living the Christian life, they wouldn't lose anything. Instead, they would find the greatest joy a human being can ever know. I had a heavy burden to minister that message to others just like myself.

As we traveled from city to city, I encountered all three of the North Central students who had given their testimony along with me that memorable day in Brother Phillips' classroom.

All three had been better students than I and had eloquently testified that God was calling them to serve Him. I always expected to hear that they had become outstanding ministers or missionaries. Ironically, one was now a policeman; another, a teacher; and the third, a businessman. Not that there is anything at all wrong with those professions.

But I was confused. Had they been called in the first place or had they simply misinterpreted what God was calling them to do? I almost felt guilty in my role as soloist with a well-known evangelist. It was everything I had ever wanted to do.

I shared this concern with David Patterson one day. "How can this be, Dave?" I asked. "I'm doing exactly what I said I wanted to do back then—singing, making records, appearing on television—reaching thousands of people for the Lord. And these other guys who were such good students aren't even in the ministry now."

Dave smiled and picked up a Bible from a nearby shelf.

"Here, Dallas, let me show you something," he said, deftly flipping the pages. "In Psalm 37:4 there is a great promise, preceded by a condition. It's this: 'Delight yourself in the Lord; and He will give you the desires of your heart' " (NASV).

"Yeah, I've read that verse before."

"But did you notice the scripture doesn't read 'His heart'? It specifically says, 'your heart.' Your desire is to sing for Him."

"That Scripture also fits neatly with Matthew 6:33, 'But seek first His kingdom and His righteousness; and all these things shall be added to you', I added.

"Right," Dave agreed. "In fact, as you put God first in every endeavor of your life, that's delighting in Him. As you consistently try to please Him, He will honor the promise part of that verse—the desires of your heart will be yours."

"Wow, that's beautiful."

"Frankly, I'm not at all surprised that God is using you, Dallas," he said, closing the Bible. "You would never have gone into some of the places where you've ministered if you hadn't felt strongly that the Lord wanted you there. And as long as you put Him first and seek to please Him, He will continue to bless you."

Dave's comments removed the sense of guilt I had carried about my former classmates. I no longer asked myself, *Why is this happening to me?* From that moment, I simply claimed Psalm 37:4 as the theme of my life.

I was delighting myself in the Lord. He was faithfully honoring that commitment by giving me the desires of my heart!

9

LET OLD THINGS
PASS AWAY

The first time Brother Dave and I met in Dallas, he assured me it wouldn't be long before I would be cutting some albums. I was definitely interested. This would represent another major step toward my goal of reaching the maximum number of people with the Gospel. Many people could be touched by a recorded message who might never attend a church or a crusade.

But, of course, I was an unknown. Nobody in the world knew Dallas Holm. Brother Dave was incredibly generous in allowing me to share in his respected, nationally-known ministry. And, sure enough, things began happening almost immediately.

The Zondervan Company expressed an interest in recording an album with me. I had never done an album with a company. There was talk of going to Nashville and using union musicians at RCA Studios. The idea appealed to me.

In March, 1970, we recorded the first album. It was entitled simply "Dallas Holm." In the meantime, I had been working on some new songs, five of which were included on the record: "I'm Telling Them Today," "He'll Still Be There," "I Won't Have to Cross Jordan Alone," "Parable of the Fig Tree," and "Choose God Today." The latter was an idea that developed as I saw the desperate need of people who were searching for answers in our crusades.

How is your heart, my friend?
Is it disturbed within?
Seems like there's no way out?
Troubled with fear and doubt?

Then why not turn to Him?
And set your life free from sin?
Your heart just seeks release
God's love and perfect peace.

So give Him your heart today,
There's nothing more to say;
Believe! It's the only way;
*So choose God today.**

The first year I traveled as a member of the crusade team sped by in record time. The apartment at 688 Broadway was home base whenever I wasn't flying off to some distant city for a crusade. We hadn't bothered to fix up the place too much since there were plans to move into more comfortable quarters in the near future.

But the pressure of living in the New York City metropolitan area, a vast melting pot of people from a great diversity of cultures, was beginning to take its toll on me. I was accustomed to the wide-open spaces of Minnesota with its abundant wildlife, its lush vegetation, its utter peace and tranquillity. I missed tracking deer in the thick pine forests or fishing the sparkling waters of the lakes and rivers, where the only sounds were the occasional cry of a wild bird or the whisper of a waterfall spilling into a quiet stream. The sounds of the teeming city were loud and discordant. I longed for the simple harmonies of nature.

Linda didn't like the city any more than I did, but she was making the best of it. She had accepted the fact that I would be away from home many weeks from Tuesday through the weekend. Being the trooper she is, she kept busy in the crusade office and in finding ways to make life easier for me when I was home.

Even so, there were times when I just couldn't stand being confined to our apartment. I had to get out and drive somewhere—usually to the end of Long Island. That was as close as I could get to a wide body of water, open sky, and a little solitude.

I wasn't the only one who was troubled by life in the metropolitan area. Being located in the place where his work with Teen Challenge was first established also created some headaches for Brother Dave. Continually, he found his energies divided between the drug rehabilitation program and his crusades. Yet, more and more he was impressed that his crusade outreach should receive his primary focus. Frequently, I heard him discussing the possibility of completely turning over the reins of Teen Challenge to his brother Don while he concentrated on the crusade ministry and his writing.

Brother Dave's best-selling book, *The Cross and the Switchblade*, had just been made into a movie starring Pat Boone. The sensational response across the country prompted even greater interest in his ministry and our travel schedule increased accordingly.

At the time, giant rallies were being held in the Los Angeles area, attracting thousands of young people burned out from the psychedelic drug culture. Hundreds of them were being converted to Christ at each of the rallies, sponsored jointly with Kathryn Kuhlman, Ralph Wilkerson, and Chuck Smith.

The early '70s were characterized by the appearance of numerous anti-war, Black power and cult groups. Many of these groups—the Black Panthers, the Brown Berets, Hare Krishna, Children of God—were coming to the West Coast meetings. The drug culture had also made its converts among California's youth. Many of these kids, high on drugs, flocked to the meetings. It made for an unusual mix in the audiences.

One night in Oakland, a city known for spawning radical groups, some six thousand people jammed the auditorium. Over a thousand of them came to the altar that night in response to Brother Dave's anointed message. He recognized that many of the kids, although committing their lives to Jesus Christ, were still high on drugs.

"You've got to realize that drug addiction is not a disease. It is sin in your life and you've got to give it up," he urged. "In fact, if you have any drugs, pills, cigarettes, or anything else on you, I want you to take it out right now and throw it up on this stage."

I don't know if Brother Dave knew what he was asking for!

All of us on stage had to duck the barrage of assorted items that came flying through the air—joints of marijuana, heroin needles, brass knuckles, chains, knives! I have never seen anything like it! After the service, we collected two big boxes full of such items.

At times Brother Dave brought kids up before the audience to tell what the Lord had done in their lives. One pretty teenage girl, tanned and blonde, came forward to share her personal testimony and to ask for prayer for her boyfriend.

She led a big husky guy on stage, with his hands extended. He took slow, halting steps, as if feeling his way across the platform. His eyes were open, but vacant. He gave every appearance of a blind person.

As the girl related his pathetic story, how he had once been a good student, an outstanding athlete, the huge audience sat spellbound. The boy was not blind. His brain had been virtually destroyed by drugs, affecting not only his vision but also his voice. He couldn't speak above a whisper. With tears streaming down her cheeks, the girl asked the crowd and Brother Dave to pray for her friend.

I stood beside Brother Dave as he prayed over the boy. I will never forget looking into those blank-looking eyes and wanting so desperately for the Lord to touch him and heal him. But there was no visible change in his condition after the prayer. Somehow, I felt he had gone too far in his waywardness. Yet, maybe the Lord saw fit to restore him in His own time. There are many things we don't know about God's timing.

However, the scene haunted me for a long time. Later, I was moved to write "Make Me a New Creature," a song that was included on my album, "Peace, Joy, and Love."

Make me a new creature,
Let old things pass away,
I hear that you can do it,
But I don't know what to say,

Fix this broken vessel,
Mold this life of clay.
Put me back together,
*Do it, Lord, today.**

In the summer of 1970, Brother Dave announced that our offices would be moving from New York City to Irvine, California. Because we traveled almost constantly, it really didn't matter where we lived as long as it was near a commercial airport. But the thought of trading the cold, bleak city for the sun and surf of California was the best news I had heard in a long time.

10

ON THE ROAD

Linda and I were singing in our hearts the day we pulled out of New York City. Our happiness was cut short when she became ill the next day. We weren't sure if it was the troublesome stomach problem again or just the excitement of the move. At any rate, we decided to rest for an extra day before traveling on.

On the way across country, we stopped off in Forth Worth where I led a service at Rosen Heights Assembly of God and visited with Pastor Stanphill. I didn't realize how much I had missed the close fellowship with Christian friends. Though barely a year had passed since I had served as youth pastor of the church, we had a lot of catching up to do. God had blessed our ministries far beyond anything either of us could have dreamed.

Linda and I settled into a typical California townhouse community in Irvine, nestled comfortably in the Los Angeles suburbs. It seemed like a dream come true—good climate, cozy apartment with pool, a more relaxed lifestyle. By contrast, living in southern California was like one long vacation. It even seemed as if here, at last, I might find some wide open spaces.

But that old nagging feeling of panic that I had suffered in the concrete jungles of New York City soon surfaced again. I longed for peace and quiet after a pressure-packed crusade trip with the clamoring crowds and the hectic pace of making flight connections.

Often, I hauled my motorcycle out in the desert, sometimes traveling for two hours or more in search of a deserted stretch of sand. But I'd be there less than five minutes when some guy would drive by in a dune buggy. I wasn't being exclusive or antisocial. It was just important for me to find some seclusion where I could recharge my spiritual batteries.

I could understand why Jesus had to get away at times. Tired and drained from the people who continually crowded around Him, demanding to be healed, to be comforted, to hear His words, He often sought a place of retreat. Sometimes, it was on or near water. "And (he) went away in the boat to a lonely place by (himself)" (Mark 6:32, NASV).

Even as a youngster, my folks allowed me to walk down to Grey Cloud Island from our house on Portland Avenue. The shoreline was marked by steep, rocky banks dotted with evergreens. Frequently, I'd sit for an hour or two just enjoying the sound of water splashing against the rocks. In years to come, the sound of water lapping against the sides of a fishing boat would provide my place of peace.

Then, only a year after we had moved to Irvine, it appeared that the ministry might relocate once again.

Brother Dave had never liked to fly. I, too, was a member of the "white knuckle" club. Following a particularly bumpy flight from Vancouver Island in British Columbia to Seattle and another on the leg home, Brother Dave announced, "Never again! You'll never find me in the air again!"

Ironically, a troublesome ulcer condition that had bothered Brother Dave for years flared up following that trip and required immediate surgery. While recovering, he had an opportunity to reflect on his fear of flying in connection with the pressing needs of the ministry. For months it had become increasingly apparent that we needed a better way to transport a greater volume of literature and more sound equipment to the larger meetings held in auditoriums and coliseums. It was more and more difficult to travel by commercial jet with that amount of materials and equipment.

During this time, Brother Dave spent hours in prayer, seeking God's direction. The solution to the problem, inspired by the Holy Spirit, was that the ministry, now known as World Challenge, should relocate somewhere in the central part of the country and should purchase a large bus.

After studying a map of the states, the city of Dallas, Texas, seemed ideal. One could travel west from Dallas for a thousand miles and be in Arizona; a thousand miles north, and be in Minnesota; or a thousand miles east and be in Florida. Yes, Dallas was the spot for us.

With a bus, we could schedule seven straight days of meetings in one state or geographical area. There would be no more hopping from one city to another for one-nighters. Also, travel by bus would be less exhausting. And, with no flight schedules to follow, we wouldn't have the hassle of rental cars, lost luggage, and other such complications.

Brother Dave, David Patterson, Richard Shultz, and I made the trip to Dallas to check out the housing situation. Though we had no pre-conceived ideas before arriving, it was decided that we would buy houses within several miles of each other in a residential area northeast of the city. We made the downpayment and flew back to prepare for the move.

Linda and I were so excited about the house, we could hardly believe it was happening to us. We had never owned a house. In fact, since I left home for Bible college, I hadn't had a place I could really call "home." For almost five years, I had been in constant motion—living first in a dormitory room, then in an apartment in Fort Worth, another in New York City, and a third in Irvine.

Now, we would have our own place with a garage where I could park the car and store my tools. Linda could decorate as much as she wanted. And we would have real neighbors— people we could get to know. Best of all, we were near the church in Fort Worth where I had served with Pastor Stanphill. I was looking forward to renewing some old friendships and making new ones.

The only note of gloom surrounding our trip

was Linda's physical condition. We had been praying for a child for some time. Just before we left California, she had some tests for pregnancy.

"Sorry, Mrs. Holm. The results of the tests are negative," the doctor reported. "You're not pregnant."

"I don't care what the doctor says, Dallas. I know I'm pregnant," Linda insisted.

To be quite honest, I wasn't sure if she was or not. But a month before we moved, she began having painful cramps and periodic bleeding. I was concerned each time I had to leave her.

The move was probably hard on her, too. Shortly after we had settled in Dallas, while I was in Oklahoma for a crusade, the phone in my hotel room rang early one morning.

"Honey, it's me," came Linda's weak voice.

"What's the matter?" I asked, sitting bolt upright in bed.

"I'm in terrible pain and I've been bleeding all night long." She sounded exhausted. "Would you please pray that it will be over soon?"

"Sure, you know I will." I prayed right over the phone, asking God to take care of Linda and bring her safely through this ordeal—whatever it was.

When I returned home, I learned about the miscarriage. Dave Patterson's wife had rushed Linda to the hospital the morning she called.

I went straight to the hospital without unpacking. When Linda saw me coming through the door, she began crying quietly.

"Oh, Dallas, I'm so sorry. I wanted so much to give you this baby."

"Come on, Linda. Don't worry, Honey. The

main thing is that you're okay."

I held her and tried to comfort her. But I couldn't find the right words. We were both disappointed. She seemed to be much more concerned for me than for herself. And I knew she was suffering both physically and emotionally. I think the emotional part was worse.

After Linda came home and began to regain her stength, we continued to pray that God would give us a child. How and when He would answer that prayer was in His hands.

A friend on the board of directors of World Challenge heard we had been praying for a child without success.

"If you want a baby so desperately, why don't you adopt one?" he suggested.

I wasn't opposed to the idea, but Linda nixed it completely. "I don't want somebody else's baby," she said firmly. "I know we can have a child and that's the baby I want. We'll just wait on the Lord. He's never late."

God's timing is always perfect. We learned, to our great joy, that Linda was pregnant. Right away, we got down on our knees and thanked Him, committing the baby she was carrying to Him.

"Father, we want this baby," I prayed, holding Linda's hand tightly. "We want this baby to be healthy. We're asking for Your protection over Linda during her pregnancy. We dedicate this child to You."

All through the long months, I prayed continually for Linda and our unborn child. In June of 1974, a blue-eyed baby girl—Jennifer

Leigh—was born, healthy and normal in every way. She was the perfect answer to our prayer. Now we were a complete family with a home of our own. We could begin to put down some real roots.

Even while there were changes on the home front, I was experiencing some other changes in the area of my recording. By 1972 I had recorded three albums on Zondervan's Singcord label— "Dallas Holm," "Just the Way I Feel It," and "For Teens Only." Creatively, I needed another outlet.

Sitting at home one day looking over my album collection, I came across a record by the Imperials on the Impact label. On the back, I noticed in the credits that the producer was Bob MacKenzie. *He must be the man I want to talk to*, I thought.

Although I'd never done that kind of thing before, I decided to give MacKenzie a call in Nashville. Being the kind of guy who just doesn't enjoy promoting himself, I had never even approached anyone about concert or church dates. So, it was pretty difficult for me to pick up the phone and dial the number for The Benson Company—but I did.

"This is Dallas Holm," I announced to the receptionist.

"Who?" she asked.

"Dallas Holm."

"Can you spell that last name?"

"H-O-L-M." *Just as I suspected, nobody has ever heard of me.*

"Well, Mr. Holm, what can we do for you?"

"I've been recording with another company

and my contract has expired. I'm interested in the possibility of recording with The Benson Company," I explained.

"I'm afraid you'll have to talk with Bob Mac-Kenzie about that," she responded, "but he's not in the office now. Would you like to leave a message?"

He won't know me either, I thought. "Well, I guess I could," I said reluctantly.

As I was giving her my telephone number, she interrupted me. "Just a minute. Bob MacKenzie just walked in the door," she said. Then I could hear her saying, "Mr. MacKenzie, I have a Dallas Holm on the line."

MacKenzie had just returned from a Christian Booksellers Convention. To my surprise, he recognized my name. While he was at the convention, he had learned about an award I had received from the National Evangelical Film Foundation as Best Contemporary Male Vocalist. We got acquainted by phone that day. Later, he flew out to Dallas where we worked out the details of a contract.

My first album on the Impact label was called "Looking Back." I wrote only one song on that album, the title tune. The following year, we cut an album entitled "Didn't He Shine." Three of my tunes appeared on that album—"Let My Light Shine," "No Good Thing Have I Done," and "Song of the Sinner."

I felt comfortable singing songs that were born out of my own personal experience. These early songs were almost all testimonial—a simple statement of where I was before Jesus saved me and what He had done for me since. The underlying message was always that "The Lord can do the same for you!"

Bob MacKenzie produced the first two albums. The third, entitled "Peace, Joy and Love," was jointly produced with Phil Johnson. A friendly, easy-going guy, Phil and I met in Nashville to make plans for the album.

I performed some songs for him that I'd written and he played a few of his own compositions. Two of his songs, "Life Never Came Easily" and "There Is a Light" were recorded on the album. I wrote five songs for the album including one which almost missed getting recorded.

Not long after I met Phil, Linda and I came back to Nashville and the Benson studios to practice some songs for the "Peace, Joy and Love" album.

"Have I heard all the new songs you've written lately?" Phil asked.

"Yeah, I think I've done 'em all," I answered.

"No more, huh?"

"Well . . ." I hedged, "I do have another one, but it's kinda like 'Peace, Joy and Love'."

"Go ahead and play it for him," Linda suggested.

"Naaw, it's kinda dumb."

"Go ahead," she continued, giggling.

Linda was so positive about Phil hearing the song, he chimed in. "Let's hear it. You can never tell."

I was kinda embarrassed about the simple little song, but I sat down at the piano and belted it out:

Jesus got a-hold of my life and He won't let me go!
Jesus got into my heart, He got into my soul!

I used to be oh so sad, But now I'm just free and glad,
'Cause Jesus got a-hold of my life and He won't let me
go!

Sometimes I remember how I used to be livin' in sin;
I tried to act happy and free but I wasn't within;
I fooled a lot of friends of mine,
They tho't I had some peace of mind,
But I never had a thing until I opened up and let Jesus
in!

Aren't you gettin' just a bit tired of foolin' around?
You try to laugh your way thro' life but you're not
gainin' ground;
Why not try the Lord today,
Just ask Him in your heart to stay,
And you'll find Jesus' love will be the greatest thing that
*you've ever found!**

"Hey, that's really good!" Phil nodded approvingly. "That one goes on the album for sure."

"See what I told you?" Linda said, grinning widely.

Phil and Linda were right. "Jesus Got Ahold of My Life" proved to be one of those simple little songs that everybody wanted to record—the Imperials, Bill Gaither Trio, Doug Oldham, Truth, and others. It was even included in songbooks and sheet music to be performed by church choirs and individuals.

That song came about one night when a fifteen-year-old girl walked forward in one of our crusades. When asked to describe her experience, she said simply, "Well, Jesus got ahold of my life and He won't let me go."

It was this song, more than any of the others, that allowed me to see songwriting as a vitally important aspect of my ministry. In retrospect, I could understand why the Lord had allowed me to spend those seven months with Ira Stanphill in Fort Worth.

Writing songs that would eventually be sung by other artists would enable me to share in their ministry and they in mine. Only God could have conceived such a plan for multiplying ministries!

*"Delight yourself in the Lord;
and He will give you the desires
of your heart."*

Psalm 37:4

11

RISE AGAIN

Annually, I was now traveling over one hundred thousand miles a year with Brother Dave. Not only were we holding crusades in the United States and Canada, but in the summer of 1972 we traveled across Europe, hitting twenty major cities in twenty-one days. Teen Challenge centers, ministering to the needs of drug users and troubled young people, had sprung up in many cities throughout Europe.

That fall we spent two weeks in Brazil. If I thought the pace in Europe was exhausting, what happened in Brazil topped it all! On our first day in Brasilia—the futuristic capital of the country, carved right out of the jungle—we had two morning services, a crusade in the afternoon, and two meetings that night. For two full weeks, that was to be the kind of schedule we would keep.

Barnard Johnson, the missionary evangelist, planned our itinerary. Johnson was considered the Billy Graham of Brazil and knew the hearts of the people. They were hungry for the

Gospel—preached, sung, any way they could get it!

Their response was incredible! Night after night we drew crowds of up to 20,000 people. The largest gathering was the final service where approximately 40,000 attended. It was worth everything to see hundreds and thousands coming forward to give their lives to Christ.

Everybody has probably wondered at one time or another what it would be like to be a movie star or a famous celebrity and be instantly recognized by the public. Because of our overwhelming reception in Brazil, Brother Dave and I briefly indulged that fantasy.

Getting to and from the meetings actually became a problem. We couldn't walk more than a few feet before we were stopped by the crowds, wanting autographs or to shake our hands. Once, someone even reached out and grabbed my hair. At times, when we got into the car to leave the services, the people pressed so hard against the windows that I was sure they would break. Driving was virtually impossible.

After two weeks of such frantic response, I decided very quickly that I didn't need that kind of acclaim. I'd leave it for the movie stars and actors. I much preferred being simply Dallas Holm—child of the King.

Following that particular tour, we all needed a change of pace. We looked forward to a few days at home with our families. But North Dallas had not turned out to be the haven we so desperately needed. It was now the fastest-growing area of the city, with housing developments and shopping centers springing up like mushrooms. Suburban commuters added to the already congested traffic. Once again, everyone in the organization felt caught up in the rat race.

Brother Dave had been fervently praying for a solution. He had long envisioned a school for young people in a ranch-type setting, where they could be trained and developed both physically and spiritually. In a way, it was the reverse of the original Teen Challenge concept. If he could reach the kids before they became hardened by drugs and life on the streets, they would have a better chance of making it.

This thinking was reinforced by a recurring vision in which he saw a series of catastrophic events coming to pass in the United States. As the American economy continued to deteriorate, he realized that a ministry such as World Challenge, which is supported largely by contributions, would be finished unless it had other means for sustaining itself. If we lived in the country, we could become self-sufficient if necessary.

The ministry purchased 360 acres of land outside Lindale, Texas, roughly eighty miles east of Dallas. The area is typical of east Texas—open pasture land, gently rolling hills, lakes, and woods—just the kind of place a guy from Minnesota could appreciate. And when we moved to Twin Oaks Ranch in the fall of 1974, just a few months after Jennifer was born, it was a lot like going home!

From the time I joined Brother Dave through 1975, I sang in crusades, accompanying myself on guitar or with an album soundtrack. But as we appeared more and more frequently before high school- and college-age kids, I began to feel that they might relate better if I was backed by a group.

Brother Dave and I were chatting one day when he changed the subject abruptly. "You didn't really ask me," he announced, "but I've been thinking we need to get a group started."

"That's really something!" I smiled. "Because I've thought about that, too."

"Why don't you work on it and see what you can come up with," he suggested.

I was both excited and hesitant about the possibility of forming a group. My experience with the rock band back in high school had caused me to be cautious about working with other people. For one thing, I wasn't sure that I could find top quality musicians who would be willing to come into an established ministry and take the backup position. It takes a lot more spiritual integrity to handle the supporting role than it does to be the guy up front.

Then, too, I wanted to be sure every member of the group would have the burden and compassion for souls that is characteristic of our ministry. A group is only as strong as its weakest link. Lack of dedication on the part of one band member could hurt the effectiveness of the entire group. "Praise," the name I had tentatively chosen for the group, must be able to live up to its name.

Having come to know Phil Johnson well as the producer of the last few albums, he was my first choice as potential member. Being a talented songwriter and vocalist himself, Phil had developed a thorough understanding of where I was professionally. He could be objective, too, sensing when a song was right for a particular album. I had come to love Phil like a brother. We think alike, we work alike—kinda easy-going and laid-back. Above all, I had complete confidence in his Christian commitment. And as a bonus, he liked to fish as much as I did!

But he declined my offer. "Thanks for considering me, Dallas," he said apologetically, "but I'm really committed to working with The Benson Company right now. My brother, Tim, and his wife, LaDonna, might be interested. They've worked with several groups and are real professionals. I'll do some checking and let you know."

Phil called his brother and sister-in-law. They agreed to fly to Twin Oaks Ranch to discuss the new group with Brother Dave and me.

I picked up Tim and LaDonna at the Dallas-Fort Worth Airport, then stopped off for lunch before proceeding to the ranch. Right away, I liked them both. LaDonna was ready to leave the secular club circuit and seemed eager to become involved with a Christian ministry. But I sensed that Tim had some reservations. Even though they were Christians, they had experienced some rough times. Maybe Tim was a little skeptical about breaking away from the only financial security they had known.

After arriving at the ranch, we settled down in Brother Dave's office to talk about our plans for the group and how it would function in the crusades.

Brother Dave has a way of cutting right through the frills and getting straight to the heart of the matter. I think he saw that Tim and LaDonna were at a crossroads—in more ways than one.

"You know, whether you join us or not is up to the Lord," he said sincerely. "I'm not real concerned about that. What does concern me is the struggle I sense you are facing. I'd like to pray with both of you."

Brother Dave walked over to the couch where Tim and LaDonna were sitting, laid hands on their heads, and began to pray.

"Lord, there is fear, doubt, and confusion here. Get hold of this young couple and transform their lives, their marriage. Let them feel Your love and Your power . . ."

At that point they wept in complete brokenness as the Presence of the Lord descended on the room. The sacred hour culminated in Tim and LaDonna recommitting their lives to the Lord and deciding on the spot to join World Challenge as part of the singing group. They knew there could be no compromise—no turning back.

Because I knew a group would soon be joining me, I had just written a song, complete with parts for other voices. Before Tim and LaDonna left that day, I sat down at the piano and played as the three of us sang. The blend was right. The chemistry was right. The spirit was right. At that moment, I just didn't know *how* right . . .

"Rise Again" had come to me uniquely. I had been alone for a couple of hours in my tiny practice studio on the ranch. It was about nine o'clock in the evening. I had been plunking on the guitar, searching for a new sound, a new approach to a song.

Finally, I did what I should have done in the first place—I prayed. As I got down on my knees, I found myself praying an unusual prayer.

Lord, this may be a strange thing to ask, but if it was You, what would You say? How would You express what You felt inside when You were dying on the cross?

Immediately, I sat down with pencil and paper and the words seemed to come from beyond and above me:

Go ahead, drive the nails in my hands;
Laugh at me where you stand;
Go ahead, and say it isn't me;
The day will come when you will see!

'Cause I'll rise again;
Ain't no pow'r on earth can tie me down;
Yes, I'll rise again;
Death can't keep me in the ground!

Go ahead, and mock my name;
My love for you is still the same;
Go ahead and bury me;
But very soon, I will be free!

Go ahead, and say I'm dead and gone,
But you will see that you were wrong.
Go ahead, try to hide the Son,
But all will see that I'm the One!

'Cause I'll come again;
Ain't no pow'r on earth can keep me back;
Yes, I'll come again;
*Come to take my people back.**

In five or ten minutes, the song was completed—both the words and the melody. I'd never written a song like that before. They just don't come that fast. I have a drawer full of uncompleted ones to attest to that fact. I realized I *didn't* write the song. The Lord wrote it. I just delivered the message.

I have heard Brother Dave say many times that God generally works through natural means, through natural processes. But to me it was a miracle as great as any I've ever seen. God actually manifested His own thoughts through a vessel of clay—like Dallas Holm!

That was just the first miracle. There were many more to come as the Lord began to use "Rise Again" in some spectacular ways.

Following a crusade one night in Bangor, Maine, we were having dinner in a restaurant when a lady walked up, introduced herself, and told us how much she enjoyed the music. Then, she related the story of a young neighbor, a 17-year-old boy with terminal cancer. The boy knew he didn't have much time to live. As his life ebbed away, he heard the song "Rise Again" and was strengthened before the end came.

"As a believer, he knew he would rise again one day—just as Jesus promised," the woman said. "Your song reminded him of the fact. He wasn't afraid to die."

I didn't know quite what to say to her. I was so deeply touched that God would use my song like that. "But that's not all," she continued. "At the funeral, they played the song and eleven of his friends gave their lives to the Lord!"

There have been cards and letters every week from people, telling of the unique way God is continuing to use "Rise Again." Most of these people testify that the song has encouraged them during a personal struggle of some kind.

With the reception of this song, I knew that our decision to form the group, "Praise," had been well-founded. Randy Adams, who had worked with World Challenge for several years, joined us as bass guitarist and vocalist. Within a few short weeks, "Praise" had become a reality.

Our first album—"Dallas Holm and Praise, Live"—rose high on airplay charts as well as sales charts. "Rise Again" was released as a single and month after month has stayed at the top of every gospel chart in the industry. Numerous groups and singers have also recorded the song.

About a year later, we decided that a drummer would give the group a fuller sound. Ric Norris, who had worked in another group with Tim and LaDonna, flew down to talk and pray about the move. He, too, stayed to join the group.

Within a year after "Praise" was formed, the Lord honored us with an assortment of awards. But our greatest joy was always in the results we saw after performing at concerts and crusades.

The first year the group was together, we were

invited to do a tour of prisons in Georgia. The music seemed to be a little tighter and Brother Dave was at his best—the old street preacher witnessing to Nicky Cruz. Except that there were as many as eight hundred guys in these meetings—tough, hardened, cynical. They were in for everything from robbery to murder. In those situations, we come on real strong, with authority and honesty. Those guys don't want to hear a lot of flowery stuff. So we don't make it easy for them.

After one service, when the invitation was given, four hundred prisoners stood to their feet and boldly walked forward in front of their buddies saying, "I want to live for the Lord for the rest of my life. And when I die, I want to know there will be no more bars and that I'll rise again."

12

IS IT TIME TO QUIT?

Several months after Jennifer was born, Linda mentioned one day that she had found a lump in her stomach just below her navel. "I can move it with my hand," she said, her brow furrowing in a worried frown. "That kinda bothers me."

"It bothers me, too," I admitted.

"Well, maybe it's just some muscles that were stretched from the pregnancy," she allowed wistfully.

"Maybe so," I responded, "but we need to have it checked out if it doesn't go away."

Little did either of us realize that problems were developing that would precipitate a major crisis in our tranquil home.

Linda had struggled with almost constant physical difficulties since our marriage. The strange stomach ailment was never far from her thoughts. The miscarriage still troubled her. And now there was the nagging worry over the mysterious lump. She was only twenty-eight and she felt that her world was coming unglued.

I was unaware of the gathering storm until one

117

afternoon after arriving home from a five-day crusade. I expected to find my usually happy, buoyant wife. Instead, she was doleful and despondent.

"Hello," Linda greeted me absently.

"Hi," I replied, surprised at her depressed countenance. "Are you okay?"

"Yeah, I guess . . . except I need to be alone for awhile." She sounded exhausted. "I need to rest."

Linda stayed in our bedroom for over an hour. I played and romped with Jennifer for awhile. When I looked in on Linda, she was lying on the bed, staring at the ceiling.

"What's wrong, Honey?" I asked, lying down beside her.

"I don't know," she said, tears gathering in her eyes. "I just don't know."

I don't know how long she had kept her feelings bottled up inside. But it was the first time she had said anything to me. We talked for hours that afternoon.

Linda seemed to be on some kind of emotional jag—with nothing either of us could put our finger on. On the surface everything was smooth—our marriage, Jennifer, the ministry, the ranch. Why, then, was she always tired? Why didn't she have the energy or even the desire to do anything, go anywhere? Why wasn't she happy? There were no answers. I just knew she hurt. And because she hurt, I hurt.

There were even times, Linda confessed, that she had felt she was losing her grasp on reality. What was the point of living in such misery? This kind of thinking was completely out of character for my normally level-headed wife.

To make matters worse, the weather in east Texas that winter was cold and cloudy, with days and days of heavy sleet, forcing Linda indoors. House-bound with a small child, and me on the road almost half the time, there was no one right there to talk with—no way to vent her frustrations.

For the first time in our marriage, we were dealing with a third party. Our marriage had never been threatened by any outside force. Now, illness, both physical and emotional, was beginning to intrude on our life together. I felt the first stirrings of fear. It crept into our marriage slowly and subtly, but it was rapidly growing to giant-sized proportions.

I was afraid to leave Linda at home alone. She was not herself. Caught up in the confusion of her own mind, I wondered if she might try to harm herself. I told myself she would never attempt a thing like that. Yet, she was really down, and I was gone so much of the time . . .

The frightening thing that was happening to Linda was not affecting my ministry, strangely enough. In fact, it seemed to strengthen it. As I felt more and more helpless to deal with her problem, I turned more often to the Lord, praying, reading His Word, seeking His will more specifically. It seemed ironic that I could successfully minister to the needs of other people when I couldn't help my wife at home.

Maybe this was God's way of giving me a nudge to consider leaving this kind of ministry for something more settled somewhere. Was the Lord trying to deal with *me* through Linda's problem? Was He trying to tell me something? Again and again, I examined my motives, my commitment, my priorities.

According to the principles by which we live on the ranch, God is first; family, second; and the ministry, third. Linda and her needs came before my ministry. So, although it would be a radical step, I approached her one day with the possibility of leaving Twin Oaks Ranch.

"How would you feel about leaving the ranch?" I asked. "I could take a church job so I wouldn't have to be away so much. We could have a normal family life . . ."

She shook her head emphatically. "No, that's not the answer."

"Why not? Wouldn't a change be good for you?"

"I know enough to realize I can't run away from this problem," she replied wisely. "It's inside me. It would be a part of me whether we stayed in this house or ran off to Timbuktu."

One Thursday night the crusade team was home. The weather was still rotten—bitterly cold days with leaden skies, threatening to drop icy rains. The usual Thursday night service was cancelled and a small informal time of communion was scheduled in its place.

The ranch families gathered quietly waiting for the serving of communion when Gwen Wilkerson began to weep. A hush fell over the room. Several people went to their knees in prayer as the Spirit of the Lord moved. Linda, too, began to weep quietly. Nothing was said. We observed communion and left for our homes.

The next morning Linda telephoned Gwen. When she called her name, Gwen interrupted.

"It was you, wasn't it? I was weeping for you last night!"

"Yes, I think so," Linda replied.

"At first I thought my tears were for some trial I might be facing, but now I realize you're the one I was weeping for."

"But I don't understand . . ." Linda confided.

"I know," Gwen sympathized, "I've been there."

"Can you tell me what's wrong with me—why I'm so miserable?"

"You're really the only person you can answer that," Gwen continued. "There are no easy answers—at least I haven't found any. I just know the Lord will be with you and can turn this time of mourning into something special. You'll see."

Gwen hadn't promised that things would get better—only that God would walk with Linda through the dark days. She wouldn't be alone.

Months passed. Linda had good days. And bad ones. At times, she felt that life had turned into a big can of worms and she was one of the wiggly creatures inside. Most perplexing was the fact she couldn't point to one specific thing and say, "*That's* the problem. *That's* what's bugging me." Her natural joy of living had been replaced, at least temporarily, by the tyrant of depression.

When the crusade team wasn't on the road, we often attended the First Baptist Church in Lindale, pastored by Bob Roberts, a dedicated man of God. Apparently, Pastor Roberts had also traveled through some deep valleys. There were some Sundays when he preached messages that spoke directly to Linda's situation.

Meanwhile, Linda lived, ate, and slept the Word. She found the book of Psalms particularly comforting during this time. She spent hours reading about David's struggles and subsequent victories.

Sometimes, as she was reading in her room, she felt the Lord speaking to her, "Linda, let's change some words in these passages and substitute your name." Where David was saying, *"I've* cried out . . ." *"I've* prayed to you" Why can't you hear *me*?" Linda made those heart cries her own.

Then, as soon as she closed her Bible, the taunting fear would return and she would plead, "Lord, are you still there?" The still, small voice within always answered tenderly, yet reprovingly, "Linda, what did you just read? Why can't you just believe?"

That assurance of God's presence helped her to move ahead slowly, clinging to the belief that He loved and cared for her and knew all about her suffering. Nor did she forget that God could deliver her from the darkness—when it was time.

One day, while reading in 2 Corinthians, she came across some verses that proved to be the light at the end of the tunnel. "Blessed be the God and Father of our Lord Jesus Christ, the Father of mercies and God of all comfort; who comforts us in all our affliction so that we may be able to comfort those who are in any affliction with the comfort with which we ourselves are comforted by God. For just as the sufferings of Christ are ours in abundance, so also our comfort is abundant through Christ" (1:3-5, NASV).

It suddenly occurred to her that what she had experienced could be used to help others dealing with similar problems. "Maybe I've gone through this so the Lord could open up my doors of compassion," she pondered.

In time a refreshing softness and a vulnerability replaced much of Linda's former proud independence. There was a new compassion and understanding for others.

She reviewed all of her past shortcomings in the light of this new discovery and recognized that some problems between herself and others might have been created because of her emotional makeup.

One woman, in particular, came to mind. After supper one evening, Linda walked around to the woman's house to chat with her.

"I don't know exactly what is wrong between us," Linda began honestly, "but I want to make things right. I'm so independent, you might have thought I was cold and unfeeling. If I've hurt you or offended you in any way, I want to apologize and ask your forgiveness."

The woman broke down weeping. "I didn't think you would ever understand how I felt," she cried. "I have always felt so isolated from people like you."

Linda felt the healing love of the Lord flowing into their relationship. And they hugged each other warmly.

This experience helped Linda to develop a high level of sensitivity to the hurts of others—

even when they are trying desperately to hide them.

There was still further healing for Linda herself. On another Thursday night, Charles Snow, who serves as ranch pastor, spoke about the dark valleys Christians sometimes find in this life. "I can't explain why they are there or why we must endure them," he confessed, "but God knows. He cares.

"Christians who have walked with the Lord for many years will tell you they have experienced these low places—these valleys," he continued. "When it seems there is no joy and no future, they have learned to trust God and found He never forsakes them! It's a situation where you have to trust God even when you don't understand—*especially when you don't understand.*"

That night, Linda stood for prayer at the close of the service. A counselor from the girls' dorm came and prayed over her. For the first time in almost a year, Linda felt the satisfying assurance that the Lord did have her life in His hands. Despite the circumstances, He had everything under control.

Even as Linda hit the road to recovery emotionally, her physical troubles were far from over. Early in 1979 she and Jennifer traveled to Minneapolis with me where I was scheduled to sing for a church convention.

The next day, Linda woke up with a sore throat and flu-like aching. A day later, the pains had localized in her stomach—that same mysterious pain—now worse than ever.

"I think I have the flu or something," Linda moaned. "This stabbing pain in my stomach doesn't ever stop."

She explained her condition to her dad, but he passed it off as nothing serious. However, the on-again, off-again pain continued to plague her even after we returned to Texas. Finally, in desperation, she had a series of X-rays made.

"It looks like your duodenum is producing too much acid," the doctor theorized after reviewing the X-rays. "What are you worried about?"

"Worried?" she repeated. "What does that have to do with it?"

"If you're overly anxious or disturbed," he explained, "that could affect the acid content of your stomach."

The pains persisted. It was then that Linda decided to see the specialist in intestinal medicine who advised her to have the major surgery. That episode had precipitated my plea to the Lord and His startling response.

Not long after Linda's surgery and dramatic recovery, I received a note in the mail from Aunt Lorena. It was just a general newsy letter asking about the family. Down at the bottom, she had added, "I've been going through some difficult emotional struggles of late. Please pray for me."

I sat for a long time looking out the window of my den as the wind blew ripples across the lake. First my mother—one of the finest Christian women I have ever known—had suffered emotional problems. Then Linda—whom no one would ever suspect could have a depressed day in her life. Now, Aunt Lorena, a woman of faith and miracles, was asking for prayer for exactly the same problem.

Could it be that one purpose in these experiences was to open up a new area of ministry? I was surely more aware of this sort of thing now that it had happened to three people in my immediate family. People are not so different. There must be many others facing dark valleys of depression.

The thought came to me that Jesus had faced this same kind of thing during his earthly life. He was misunderstood. He was rejected by even his closest friends. He knew those dark, lonely feelings. At one point in the Garden, he had even prayed, "If there's any other way, let this cup pass from me." Surely, He was in the darkest valley then.

Jesus knows your hurt. Just that knowledge alone can sustain a person in crisis. He, alone, understands better than any other because *He has felt all the pain there is!* That is still one of the greatest mysteries in the Bible—that God took on the likeness of man—to feel, to know, to suffer, to redeem—*when He didn't have to.*

As the Lord made these truths real in my own life, they naturally began to surface in my music. The album, "All That Matters," grew out of this whole series of events. And the song, "Jesus Knows Your Hurt," carried the message for my mom, Aunt Lorena and Linda.

The pain some people bear
No one would believe;
The hurt that's sometimes there
makes it hard to see

That in the darkest hour
There is still a way;
Listen to these simple words, I say:

Jesus knows your hurt,
Jesus feels your pain;
Jesus knows just how you feel,
'cause He's felt just the same.
Jesus knows your need
better than you do;
Just hold on to Jesus,
He's holding on to you!

Sometimes you feel alone,
Does He really care?
Has He left you all alone,
and does He hear your pray'r?
Well, He has never left you or forsaken you one day;
Listen to these simple words, I say:

Jesus knows your hurt,
Jesus feels your pain;
Jesus knows just how you feel,
'cause He's felt just the same.
Jesus knows your need
better than you do;
Just hold on to Jesus,
*He's holding on to you!**

13

ALL THAT MATTERS

Several years back, Brother Dave and I did a camp meeting at Carlinville, Illinois, for the Assemblies of God. The denomination operates a radio station there, where I was interviewed by Dale Lidstrom, a gospel disc jockey.

A personable man, Dale posed an interesting question. "Dallas, have you ever wondered where music originated?"

"No, I guess I haven't," I replied.

"Well, I've thought about it a lot," he continued enthusiastically. "After you get past all the different styles of music and the thousands of years of recorded time, you're faced with the fact that music was created by God. After all, He's the Creator of heaven and earth and everything therein. Right?"

I nodded. There didn't seem to be much to add.

"Okay, if that's the case then, what was the original purpose of music?" The guy was really wound up and didn't pause for my answer. "Without question, I think it was to glorify the

Lord. It was something He created whereby His creatures could communicate with Him."

"Right," I agreed. But it was his next question which set me thinking and pondering for weeks to come.

"Where are you now, Dallas?" he probed. "What are you saying with your music in view of what music was intended to do?"

I couldn't get away from that haunting question. I had written either songs of testimony about what the Lord had done in my life or songs of appeal to unbelievers to accept Christ. Yet, for weeks prior to this rather one-sided interview, I sensed a definite change coming. I felt I had reached a turning point in my songwriting and now it was time to move on. But where?

Suddenly, it seemed clear that instead of singing about problems or asking questions in my songs, I could simply invite the presence of the Lord into the lives of my listeners. I remembered that John 12:32 had something to say about that. "And I, if I be lifted up from the earth, will draw all men unto me."

If I invited God's presence into a concert or album, I wouldn't need to remind people that Jesus is the solution to their problems. The Holy Spirit would do that in His own perfect way.

From that point on, I decided to start singing to the Lord instead of to the people. I made it a point to glorify Him in every way I could. That decision spawned such songs as "He Means All to Me," "The Song of Love," and "Here We Are."

Some of my songs—like "Rise Again"—have

come in unusual ways. For the most part, though, they have come while I was riding down the highway on the bus headed for a crusade, or in the studio.

"Tell Everyone" and "What Will You Do?" were written in a motel in Opp, Alabama, where we had just held a one-day crusade with tremendous results. When I returned to my room that night, I was on a spiritual high. I felt the Lord's presence in a very special way.

I began thinking about the Lord, about His love, and how good He had been to us. It was as though, for a brief moment, I could comprehend His love. I realized that, in the midst of all His power and glory with all of creation to look upon, He was infinitely more concerned with one human soul than with all the glories of the universe.

Before I realized it, I found myself praying, *Lord, tell me again what You want to say, just like you did in "Rise Again."*

I was surprised at my own words. A song like "Rise Again" would probably never happen again. I began to feel the same hesitancy I had felt while writing that song. I thought to myself, *Does anyone have the right to assume what God would say?* But I knew I had to obey what the Lord was impressing upon me.

As I prayed, broken before the Lord, I sensed the words coming from deep inside me. I knew it was a song everyone—believer and non-believer alike—needed to hear. I knew if the Lord Himself got up before a crowd and sang to them, it would be the message He was giving me at that moment:

Tell ev'ryone that I love them;
Tell ev'ryone that I care.
Tell ev'ryone I want to see them;
Tell ev'ryone they can share

in the things I've prepared.
No one would believe;
All I have they can share
    if only they'll receive Me.

Tell ev'ryone that I'm coming;
Tell ev'ryone that it's soon;
tell all who listen get ready
I've still got plenty of room.

We will meet in the air,
Then we'll go away
To a place I've prepared.
There you'll always stay with Me.

Then, before the ink was dry on the verses, came the words to the chorus—an appeal to people hesitating about making a decision for the Lord.

I want you all to come.
I want you all to see;
Oh, how I've waited for you to come to Me.
I want you all to be happy;
I want you all to be free;
*I want you all to spend all of time with Me.**

Richard Dresselhaus had long since resigned as pastor of Summit Avenue Assembly of God to assume another pastorate in San Diego. Recently, after teaching a seminar near Lindale, he

---

decided to drop off at Twin Oaks Ranch and visit Brother Dave, Linda, and me. It had been some years since we had seen him.

Linda and I—like a couple of school kids—gave our former pastor the grand tour of the ranch. Then, we went back to our house to chat before supper.

That year, the group and I had received four different Dove Awards—Song of the Year for "Rise Again," Songwriter of the Year, Male Gospel Vocalist of the Year, and Mixed Gospel Group of the Year.

Because of a concert in Savannah, Georgia, I was unable to attend the ceremonies in Nashville. Phil Johnson, as our producer, accepted the awards in our place. He later sent them to the ranch where Linda placed them on top of our stereo/TV cabinet.

Linda and I enjoyed our visit with Pastor Dresselhaus, laughing and talking about old times. It seemed as if he remembered every detail of leading me to the Lord, marrying us, and watching us grow spiritually.

"Who would have ever thought that God would have done all these beautiful things in your lives?" he said.

"Certainly not I," I agreed.

"Nor I," Linda smiled.

"As you get on down the road in your ministry," he remarked, "one of the most rewarding things is to lead somebody to the Lord and then step back and watch them grow. If and when they ever go into the ministry, the blessing just mushrooms. It's kinda like fathering children in the Lord. It's really something you can take a lot of fatherly pride in . . . I'm just so proud of you both."

Linda and I were so appreciative of people like Pastor Dresselhaus who all along had shown their concern and support. There were others too, like Ira Stanphill and certainly Brother Dave. I felt it was people like that who had a large share in any success I had in the ministry.

Not long after Pastor Dresselhaus' visit, the crusade team—Brother Dave, Praise, and I—were in the state of Washington for crusades in Seattle and Tacoma. One night my throat tightened up and I had great difficulty singing. The final night, though, everything went well and I didn't think anymore about it.

Dad had retired from his long-time job with the dairy and, with Doug living in Corpus Christi and me in Lindale, my parents decided to move to Texas. So, instead of returning to the ranch with the guys, I flew back to Minnesota to help my folks pack and make the long trip.

Driving the rental truck south, I felt the throat problem returning. It grew sorer and sorer, finally winding up in a bad case of laryngitis.

That was nothing new. I had had laryngitis before. But it is a nagging worry to a singer. My first impulse was to check the calendar to see how many days I had left to get well before the next concert. After about a week, the worst of the soreness disappeared.

But I was left with lingering hoarseness and a hacking cough. I couldn't sing with the openness and power I once had—especially when I went for the higher notes. I choked off and couldn't push it out.

I kept telling myself, *I'll get over it sooner or later. I'll just have to be patient.* But each time I thought I had finally gotten past the problem, the laryngitis returned. That happened three times in succession. I couldn't shake the problem.

As the laryngitis came and went, I discovered I wasn't as happy and contented as I usually am. Singing was such a major part of my life and all of a sudden I was having great difficulty with it. What was worse, there seemed to be nothing I could do to change the situation. Through those months of vocal problems, it seemed there wasn't a day I didn't worry about my voice. It hung over me constantly like a dark cloud.

My mood was further darkened when I learned Brian Daniel, an ordained minister who drove Brother Dave's bus, was leaving the organization to pastor a church. Since the group had formed, we had gotten a second bus which Ric drove for the most part.

Brian had a varied background before he came to the Lord: truck driver, rodeo circuit "bronco buster," carpenter. He had been with the ministry over five years.

During that time, we had become close friends—primarily because of our mutual interest in hunting and fishing. We both used the outdoors as our release valve from the pressure of traveling. Brian was such a refreshingly honest guy, I grew to love and appreciate him in a special way. I knew I would miss our trips to the woods and lakes of east Texas, when he was gone. If my vocal problems were like a dark cloud, losing my best friend was like the rain itself.

Finally, in February 1980, I went to a throat specialist. I had heard enough about singers developing nodules on their vocal chords to produce a little fear in the back of my mind.

The doctor poked and prodded and crammed all manner of tiny metal gadgets down my throat. Then he pronounced me fine. No nodules on the vocal chords.

"But why all the trouble with the throat?" I asked, perplexed with his simple findings.

"Do you have any allergies?" he questioned.

"I've always had hay fever," I answered.

"Ah-ha," he said. "It's probably a drainage problem then. Too much sinus drainage is probably irritating the vocal chords."

I wasn't really satisfied with that answer. I'd lived at the ranch over five years and had never had any trouble like that before. Why now?

There wasn't a day that went by that I didn't think about the difficulty. I listened to some of my older albums and thought, *I was singing better then than I am now.* Suddenly, there were songs I'd written that I couldn't sing without straining my throat.

At times I came off the platform after a concert, mumbling to myself, "I just don't know what the problem is. I just can't seem to get it out anymore."

"Hey, you're fine," the guys in the group always assured me. "You're sounding as good as ever."

But I knew better. The laryngitis continued to plague me. Eventually, I developed a high fever which landed me in bed and forced the cancellation of a concert—a rare turn of events for me.

When that happened, Brother Dave came over to the house.

"You know, Dallas," he said, after praying over me, "I've noticed you've been straining on some of the songs lately."

I nodded, unable to speak above a whisper.

"I think you're worried that if you can't sing, you'll be out of a job," he said, coming to the point quickly. "As far as I'm concerned you've always got a job here. If you can't sing, you can always do something else."

"That's good to hear," I croaked.

He smiled. "I want you to have another doctor check your throat," he suggested. "Maybe you ought to take some time off—three months, six months—maybe even a year. And I don't want you to worry about it. There's no problem."

No doubt I had been worried about my place in the ministry. Although I had been with Brother Dave for ten years and was a vice president and member of the board, I realized nobody was indispensable.

It occurred to me that the Lord might be making me eat my words. Down through the years I have claimed that singing is not so special. I'm certainly not any better than anybody else because I can sing. *If I woke up tomorrow and couldn't sing*, I would tell myself, *I'd be just as happy.*

That's easy to say when your voice is sounding great and there's no pain in your throat. But all of a sudden my voice had gone sour on me and I wasn't happy—not at all. It was an ironic twist of fate, I thought.

Months before, Linda had come through a dark valley. I never expected to face a similar struggle. Yet here I was—worried, frustrated, depressed. Little cracks of insecurity appeared where I thought I had always felt perfectly secure. I had never had a problem with my voice. I had always been able to sing whatever and whenever I wanted to sing. But the hoarseness persisted and the Lord hadn't seen fit to remove the ailment even though I'd asked repeatedly.

I have said that God doesn't always answer our prayers immediately. Sometimes He allows us to endure trials so we can learn to trust Him more. I have said I believe the faith that really pleases the Lord is not just the faith that expects miracles—it is the kind of faith that, even in the midst of our trial and confusion, says *I love You, trust You, and believe in You, no matter what happens!* Yet, here I am in the middle of my trial and some disturbing thoughts have entered my mind. *Do some things just happen? Is God really aware of my condition or is this something that will work itself out?* And then the most shocking question of all—*Do I believe for myself what I have always preached to others?*

Stunned by the impact of my conflicting thoughts, I turned in complete submission to the Lord. *Whatever You want, Lord,* I prayed, *whatever You want.* I began to feel again His calming presence. He was more aware of my problem and what it might mean to my life and ministry than I could ever be. I saw, too, that my happiness doesn't depend upon my ability to sing. My happiness, joy, and contentment in life come primarily from my relationship with Him and not from anything I *do.*

In the months that followed, my voice began

showing gradual signs of improvement. In time, I knew it could be back to normal. At least I hoped and prayed that it would. My desire—first and foremost—has always been to serve the Lord through music.

But I came to a solid decision. Whatever comes, whether I wind up singing and writing songs for the rest of my life, or baling hay at Twin Oaks Ranch in Texas, the Lord comes first. As never before, my delight is in Him.

I sing songs of joy,
I sing songs of pain,
Songs that will move the soul;
But if I should never sing them again,
Here's something you've got to know:

All that matters in this life below
is not what you are or how much you know;
All the world's knowledge can make the mind smart,
But the diff'rence is made in the heart.*

EPILOGUE

It's rather ironic, I suppose, that the end of this story is really the beginning of another . . .

Even as this book was coming off the press, I was in the process of making one of the most important decisions of my life. Sometimes, it seems, just when you think you've got the whole thing figured out and you know what it is you're supposed to do, the Lord comes along and stirs your nest.

In July of 1980 I felt led of the Lord to leave the ministry with which I had been involved for over ten years, and go out on my own with Dallas Holm and Praise. Only days before making this decision, I had told someone in an interview that I had no plans for ever going out on my own. (Proof once again that our ways are not necessarily His ways!)

Leaving the David Wilkerson ministry was sort of like leaving home. You don't really *want* to but there comes that time when you know you *have* to!

It was a little scary at first. For ten years I had known exactly what my ministry was, I had had a regular income, and I had been part of a larger group of people. Consequently, there had been a very strong sense of security.

Now I wasn't totally sure where the Lord would take me. I knew I would be forfeiting a certain amount of financial security. In a sense, we would be starting afresh.

Suddenly, as I reflected on the experiences encountered and lessons learned in the pages of this book, I could once again see the hand of God carefully weaving His master plan.

One of the main things Linda and I have learned in the past few years is to trust and depend on the Lord even when we can't see what He is doing. Had we not gone through the things we have and learned to trust Him like we do, we would never have known the joy and peace that we are experiencing even now as we begin this story . . .

Pray for us.

Dallas Holm & Praise
Box 1000
Lindale, TX 75771

*"Delight yourself in the Lord;
and He will give you the desires
of your heart."*

Psalm 37:4

My brother, Doug, and I---in hot water!

Doug's birthday; sittin' on the fence; Christmas with Grandma and Grandpa

Dad, me, Mom, & Doug

MY FAVORITE THINGS
Linda, Jennifer, and fishin'

Some of the kids at Rosen Heights---and with the Wilkerson crusade in New York City. (That's David Wilkerson, far right.)

Ric, Randy, LaDonna, Tim

DALLAS HOLM AND PRAISE

Tim Johnson (keyboards), Dallas, Randy Adams (bass), Ric Norris (drums)

Praise poses beside Holm away from home